BEDTIME STORIES

FOR ADULT

VAGUS NERVE STIMULATION FOR INSOMNIA

Relaxing lullabies to reduce stress, anxiety & panic attacks. Natural healing to ensure a good night rest and fall asleep quickly

Kirsten Wallace

Table of Contents

Introduction

Sleep, as necessary as it is, is also incredibly fickle. It is incredibly easy to disrupt sleep in endless fashions, from anxiety and intrusive thoughts to problems with the lifestyle that you are living and about a million in-between possibilities. You know that you are not getting that rest that your body needs, and when that happens, everyone suffers.

Vagal nerve stimulation has an assortment of impacts on rest and attentiveness, which include: improved daytime readiness and rest structural changes, diminished REM (Rapid eye movement) rest and expanded renewals, wake after rest onset, and stage NREM (non-rapid eye movement) 1 sleep.

Incitement is additionally connected with diminishes in wind stream and exertion matching with VNS initiation. It would be ideal if you note that a sleep concentrate in instances of suspected sleep apnea ought to be performed before embedding the VNS into the person.

When you remember the information that will provide in this book, you will be able to help yourself. You will be able to ensure that you can take care of everything that you need. You will remember that you will be able to fix yourself, your sleep, and everything else that comes with it. You will know that you will have the tools that you will need to defeat your insomnia and ensure that you do get the rest in your life.

Remember the information that has been provided to you. Do not forget the fact that the secret to a good day is to have a good night and do not forget just how heavy that a lack of sleep that is healthy and restful can put on your mind. Do not forget that you are the only one responsible for the sleep that you need and that you can help promote and facilitate it with ease. Do not forget that you can better cope with the stressors of your life. Do not forget that your mindset is just as important as your physical health.

When you can remember that the body and mind are one, you can ensure that you keep that comfort that your body needs. You can ensure that you can provide everything that you need to get the sleep that will keep your body healthy.

From here, all that is left to do is to change your habits for the better. If you want the fullest effects of everything, from the exercises that you are going through to the sleep that you are getting to the way that you are thinking, you must ensure that you embrace everything that this book has offered you. This means that you need to keep up with it. You need to remember that these changes that we're encouraged to you are lifestyle changes. They are ways of life. They are not simply used for a week and magically, for life, fix your sleep problems; rather, they must be used regularly to continue to see the benefit.

Chapter 1: Vagus Nerve Stimulation

The vagus nerve functions as the body's superhighway, taking information between the brain and the internal organs and controlling the body's reaction in times of relaxation and rest. The huge nerve originates from the brain and branches from numerous directions to the throat and chest. It's accountable for activities like carrying sensory data from the epidermis of the ear, so controlling the muscles you use to eat and talk and affecting your immune system.

Functions of Vagus Nerve

The vagus nerve provides the maximum extensive supply of these cranial nerves. Its own pharyngeal and laryngeal branches carry motor impulses into the pharynx and larynx; its own coronary branches act to bring down the rate of the pulse; its own bronchial division functions to constrict the bronchi; along with its own esophageal branches that command involuntary muscles at the esophagus, gut, gallbladder, pancreas, along with the small intestine, triggering peristalsis and gastrointestinal secretions.

Vagus nerve stimulation, where the heart is stimulated with pulses of power, is occasionally employed for patients with epilepsy or even depression that's otherwise untreatable; this procedure continues to be investigated for ailments like Alzheimer's disease along with migraine.

The vagus nerve delivers parasympathetic motor fibers into each of the organs (except the adrenal glands) in the neck to the next sector of the rectal colon. The vagus also modulates several skeletal muscles, such as:

- Cricothyroid muscle
- Levator veli palatini muscle
- Salpingopharyngeus muscle
- Palatoglossus muscle
- Palatopharyngeal muscle
- Superior, middle and inferior pharyngeal constrictors
- Muscles of this larynx (speech).

This means that the Vagus nerve is liable for such diverse activities as heart rate speed, gastrointestinal peristalsis, perspiration, plus quite a few muscle movements in the gut, as well as speech (through the recurrent laryngeal nerve).

Stimulation of the cervix uteri (like in certain healthcare procedures) may result in some vasovagal reaction.

The vagus nerve plays a part in satiation after food ingestion. Knocking out vagal nerve cells was proven to trigger hyperphagia (significantly increased food consumption).

Vagus Nerve and The Heart

Parasympathetic innervation of the heart is partly controlled by the vagus nerve and can be shared with the thoracic ganglia. Vagal and spinal column ganglionic nerves interrupt the lowering of the heart rate. The right vagus branch innervates the sinoatrial node. In healthy men and women, the parasympathetic tone from these types of resources is well-matched to tone. Hyperstimulation of parasympathetic influence boosts bradyarrhythmia. After being hyper-stimulated, the abandoned vagal branch divides the heart into the atrioventricular node's conduction block.

A neuroscientist named Otto Loewi initially revealed that nerves secrete compounds known as neurotransmitters that have impacts on receptors in target cells. In his experimentation, Loewi electrically stimulated the vagus nerve of a frog's heart, which slowed the heart. He then took the fluid out of the heart and moved it into another frog's heart with no vagus nerve. The other heart slowed down with no electric stimulation.

Loewi explained the material introduced by the vagus nerve as vaguest, which afterward was discovered to be acetylcholine. Drugs inhibit the muscarinic receptors (anticholinergics), for example, atropine, along with scopolamine, are known as vagility since they inhibit the activity of the vagus nerve in the heart, gastrointestinal tract, liver, and other organs. Anticholinergic drugs raise heart rate and, therefore, are utilized when treating bradycardia.

Physical and Emotional Effects

Excessive activation of the vagal nerve through psychological stress can be a parasympathetic overcompensation that causes a powerful feeling in the nervous system reaction connected with anxiety. It may also bring about vasovagal syncope because of a sudden reduction in coronary output, inducing cerebral hypoperfusion. Vasovagal syncope affects young children and girls over other groups. Additionally, it may result in temporary loss of bladder management under moments of intense anxiety.

Research has revealed that girls who had a spinal cord accident can undergo climaxes through the vagus nerve, which may go to your uterus along with the cervix to your brain.

Insulin signaling activates the adenosine triphosphate (ATP)-sensitive potassium (KATP) channels from the arcuate nucleus, reduces AgRP discharge, and through the vagus nerve, which contributes to reduced sugar production from the liver by diminishing gluconeogenic enzymes like Phosphoenolpyruvate Carboxykinase, and 6-phosphatase.

Vagus nerve structure and function

The term "vagus" means drifting in Latin. This is a really appropriate title since the vagus nerve is the strongest. It runs all of the ways from the brain stem into a part of the colon.

The sensory acts of the vagus nerve are broken up into two elements:

- Somatic parts: All these are sensations felt in by nerves in the skin.

- Visceral parts: All these are sensations felt in the organs of the body.

Sensory Functions of The Vagus Nerve Comprise:

Providing somatic feeling information for the skin behind the ear, and the external portion of the ear, and also specific areas of the neck provide visceral feeling information for your larynx, lungs, esophagus, trachea, heart, and the majority of the gastrointestinal tract plays a small part in the sense of taste close to the base of the tongue

Motor functions of the vagus nerve include:

- Triggering muscles in the pharynx, larynx, and the palate, that's the area close to the rear of the roof of the mouth

- Triggering muscles in the heart, which helps to reduce resting heart rate

- Triggering involuntary contractions from the gastrointestinal tract, including the stomach, esophagus, and the majority of the intestines, that enable food to move throughout the digestive tract

Parasympathetic Roles

From the thorax and gut, the vagus nerve may be the primary parasympathetic outflow into the heart and also organs that are failing.

Heart

Cardiac branches start from the thorax, dispersing parasympathetic innervation into the sino-atrial and atrioventricular nodes of the heart.

These branches cause a decrease in the resting heart rate. They're always busy, making a rhythm of 60-80 beats per second. When the vagus nerve is lesioned, the resting heart rate can be approximately 100 beats per second.

Gastro-Intestinal System

The operation of this Vagus nerve-wracking is always to stimulate smooth muscle contractions and glandular secretions in those organs. By way of instance, at the gut, the vagus nerve increases the amount of gastric emptying and also stimulates acid generation.

Sensory roles

You will find visceral and also somatic parts in the sensory role of the vagus nerve-racking.

Somatic identifies sensation from skin and muscles. That is given by the auricular nerve, which innervates the skin from the anterior portion of the external auditory canal along with the outer ear.

Viscera sensation is that done by the organs of the human body.

The innervation of the vagus nerve:

- Laryngopharynx -- via the internal laryngeal nerve.

- Heart -- via nerve branches of the vagus nerve.

- Superior facet of the larynx (preceding rectal folds) -- through the internal laryngeal nerve.

- Gastrointestinal tract (in the splenic flexure) -- via the terminal branches of the vagus nerve.

Vagus Nerve Stimulation and its Benefits

Vagus Nerve stimulation might be the secret to improving your quality of life. Inflammation may be the underlying reason for the majority of diseases because the immune system starts an inflammatory reaction to safeguard tissues if it senses danger. But, discovering the very first cause of this redness may end up being a significant challenge.

The Vagus Nerve links to a number of body systems and features a very substantial effect on systemic inflammation and general wellbeing.

Assessing the Vagus Nerve and its Functions

Reports assess the reason why the Vagus Nerve is crucial and the way it works to contribute to health, for example:

- Exactly why the Vagus Nerve is very important

- The way the Vagus Nerve affects health

- Signs and signs of Vagus Nerve malfunction

- Vagus Nerve stimulation and its particular benefits

- A significant note on gluten and also the Vagus Nerve

Exactly why the Vagus Nerve Is Significant

Produced from the Latin word vagus, this means "to roam," so the Vagus Nerve is justifiable for its name. The Vagus Nerve originates at the cerebellum and brainstem, winds through the entire body, and branches several areas to innervate all the vital organs:

- Pharynx

- Larynx

- Heart

- Esophagus

- Gut

- Small intestine

- Large intestine upward to the splenic flexure

This elongated reach results in the Vagus Nerve playing a part in roles like the taste, swallowing, speech, heartbeat, digestion, and excretion.

The Vagus Nerve functions as an integral part of the nervous system, or PNS, that will be related to bodily activities categorized as "rest and eat up. "

As its title suggests, the PNS focuses primarily on soothing down the body and digesting food to renew the entire body's energy source as one of its purposes. To make this happen, the Vagus Nerve communicates using its associated organs by discharging a neurotransmitter is known as acetylcholine that can help regulate blood pressure, blood sugar balance, heart rate, digestion, breathing and speaking, perspiration and kidney function, bile discharge, saliva secretion, and female fertility, along with climaxes.

The Vagus Nerve also supports hormones throughout the entire human anatomy. Insulin reduces glucose release from the liver to invigorate the Vagus Nerve, where the thyroid gland, T3, stimulates the Vagus Nerve to maximize desire, including the creation of ghrelin. Ghrelin also arouses the Vagus Nerve to boost appetite.

Vagus Nerve work is indispensable to the discharge of oxytocin, testosterone, and vasoactive intestinal peptide. The creation of human growth hormone-releasing hormone, GHRH, and also the stimulation of adrenal hormone such as converting vitamin D 3 into active vitamin D are additionally trusted to the Vagus Nerve.

The Way the Vagus Nerve Impacts Physical and Mental Wellness

The Vagus Nerve affects organs in the central nervous system, or CNS, that is made up of the brain and spinal cord, so it's crucial not to forget that the Vagus Nerve is suspended in the brain stem and cerebellum. Optimal Vagus Nerve features, or "high vagal tone indicator," is related to healthy social interactions, positive emotions, and improved physical health and fitness. People with low vagal tone indicators experience depression, heart attacks, loneliness, unwanted feelings, and stroke.

Brain wellness and gut health affect one another, and also, the Vagus Nerve is the connection between them both. Even the vagal tone indicator is looked at as your human body's "gut feeling," which is pulled straight into the brain and also produces a feedback loop of greater positivity or even maybe more negativity.

Emerging studies indicate the vagal tone indicator is set by signs discharged from the immune system called cytokines. Research is underway to comprehend how better stimulating the Vagus Nerve delivers the capacity for treating inflammatory illnesses, such as rheumatoid arthritis symptoms, without pharmaceutical medication.

Vagus nerve stimulation (VNS) transmits ordinary, moderate rhythms of electric energy into the brain via the vagus nerve, by way of a system that's very similar to a pacemaker. There's not any physical participation of the brain within this operation, and patients don't generally have that stimulation. It's crucial to remember the VNS is an alternative option restricted by choosing people who have epilepsy or treatment-resistant depression.

Chapter 2: A Christmas Story

Once upon a Christmas holiday, there was a low-income family. There were a mother and father and two minimal ones. The family was inferior to the point that they had no spot to live except for in an old vehicle out in the back lanes. Individuals that knew about them didn't comprehend their circumstance since they didn't attempt to understand. The town individuals would call them names and point fingers at them.

One day the two minimal ones went up to their mom and father and asked, "For what reason do we live in a vehicle and not in a house? For what reason aren't we in school?" They had tears moving down their cheeks.

The two parents sat them down, "Dear kids, we don't have these things since we don't have employment. We have attempted to cling to our employments. It appears the individuals we generally help are excessively stressed.

They stress over how individuals look and not merely the work. We have minimal expenditure to purchase new garments. We've attempted to approach individuals for help; however, we can't get it.

That is the reason we aren't ready to have the things that others have." The kids comprehended and didn't ever ask again. Their folks sent them to the vehicle to hit the sack. It was the following day, and it was the mothers to go out and check whether anybody would contract her.

There was no karma by any stretch of the imagination. So, the mother and father plunged down and discussed what they could do about the issues and make their kids' blessing from heaven. That day a rich man, by the name of Mason, came into town.

He wanted that one day he could have youngsters. He contemplated receiving kids sometime in the future. He wasn't precisely sure what to do. Joe showed at least a bit of kindness of gold. He never considered himself; he was continually considering others and what they need.

As he was driving along this night, he saw a group of four. They were picking through the trash for nourishment; to keep warm, they remained by a flaring trash canister. He saw that they were wearing clothes. Their appearances were messy, and their hair was messed seriously.

Mason strolled by and contemplated what he ought to do. The following day the mother and father went out to search for work. It was approaching Christmas Eve, and they needed to attempt to look for some employment again before everything had shut. Entryway to entryway, they went. Wherever they went, they were booted out, dismissed, and entryways closed forcefully.

Mason was to observe this, and he felt grave. He couldn't accept how egotistical the individuals who lived nearby were. Mason needed to take care of business. He thought for some time, and afterward, he understood this family had something that he needed, and that was a family. Joe had something that they needed.

This was home. So, Mason chose he would move toward them. "I have been watching you since I came into town. I have seen you and your significant other attempting to bring home the bacon, yet when you have not had the option to look for some employment, you can't bring back the bacon that way. I've been thinking for a couple of days. I have something you need. This is home. You have something that I need.

This is a family. I need to welcome you to my home for Christmas. After Christmas, on the off chance that you need to be a part of my family or should I say on the off chance that I could be a part of your family, we can talk about it" The family stated, "Yes!" After Christmas, they all concurred that they should turn into a family. The youngsters started school. The guardians found a new line of work, and they lived gladly ever after.

Alexander

Sometime in the distant past, there was a mouse named Alexander, and a Dog called Butch. The two of them lived in a two-story house with a group of seven. Alexander lived in the storm cellar without anyone else's input. Alexander was a forlorn mouse. He couldn't converse with anybody.

The little mouse regularly went upstairs to see what was happening. Butch was a tremendous bull Dog, yet he was an inviting canine to everybody. He was light darker with a short tail. One night as the Simpson family was watching films, Butch chose to go down to the storm cellar and look at it.

Alexander looked as Butch sniffed around his modest home. Butch, at last, saw Alexander shaking in one corner of the lounge chair. Butch gradually climbed to him. Butch took a gander at Alexander. He asked, "Who are you?" Alexander's mouth was all the way open. He was stunned to hear this animal conversing with him.

Did Alexander say in a temperamental voice? "My name is Alexander." Butch took a gander at Michael and let him know, "Don't be apprehensive." Butch began conversing with Alexander about where he originated from and the spots he has been.

Alexander felt calm as Butch began conversing with him about his life, weeks passed by as Alexander and Butch became more acquainted with one another. Both Michael and Butch started to hanging out at Alexander's place in the storm cellar. From that point, they became companions, after such a large number of long stretches of being separated from everyone else. Alexander's petitions were replied. He was upbeat; he found a companion to converse with.

Chapter 3: Guided Meditation to Help You Relax

You are about to begin a guided meditation, which will help you release stress and tension so that you can fall into a deep, peaceful sleep. Before we begin, please get comfortable. You should be lying down in a safe, warm place where you will not be interrupted, and you can remain sleeping when the meditation is complete. We'll start by bringing the awareness fully into the body, and then we'll use this awareness to bring about a completely relaxed state of mind from which you will drift, easily, into deep, good quality sleep.

These next thirty minutes are for you. This is your time. There is nothing you need to do; nowhere you need to be; no one you need to be.

Let the rest of the day up until this point drift away. Whatever you've done today, and whatever you've felt; the conversations you've had with the people you've seen; all of it begins to fade away. Visualize yourself walking into this room, lying down and closing your eyes, coming to this moment.

Know that you deserve this time. By listening to this recording, you are showing yourself and your body, love, and care, and by offering this to yourself, you will be better able to offer love and care to others.

Now take a deep breath in through the nose and sigh the breath out through the mouth.

Again, inhale deeply through the mouth and exhale through the nose.

One more time.

Bring your right hand to your belly; rest it gently on your lower abdomen. And then bring your left hand to your chest. Take a deep breath into your right hand, filling your belly up like a balloon, as much as you can. And then exhale out of your right hand, so your belly falls.

Again: Inhale right hand. Exhale right hand—three more times. Inhale right hand, belly rises. Exhale right hand, belly falls. See if you can fill the belly with a little bit more air on every inhale, and then with the exhales, pull the abdominal muscles back towards the spine. Inhale right hand, exhale right hand. Inhale, exhale.

And then inhale into the left hand. Deep inhale, filling the whole chest with the breath. And exhale out of the left hand - chest falls. Inhale left; exhale left—three more times. Inhale left; breathing rises to the collar bone. Exhale. Inhale left; exhale left. Inhale, exhale.

Then we'll start to connect the two. On the next breath, inhale deeply into the right hand - belly rises - and then the left side - chest increases. Exhale left hand - chest falls - and right hand - belly falls. Inhale right; left. Exhale left, right. Take ten more breaths like this. Deep, full breaths.

[Pause; 40 seconds for deep breaths and music]

That's great.

Now let go of control of the breath.

Notice how the breath feels in the body. Take a few moments to observe the rhythm of your breath, and notice where it goes in the body - whether it feels like the air is traveling down to your abdomen, or moving into the ribcage and then back up and out, or staying even higher up in the chest. Don't try to control it - there's no right or wrong. Just notice the pattern and the depth of the breath, without judgment.

[Allow one or two minutes for unguided breathing here]

Continue with this gentle, uncontrolled, unhurried breath. Your body knows how to do this.

Your body knows how to support you throughout the day and throughout the night; when to breathe and how fast, how deeply. Your muscles, bones, and organs know how to carry you through the movements and interactions you have in your life. And your body knows, innately, how to carry you into a comfortable, deep sleep. As your eyelids grow a little heavier, trust the knowledge of your body. There is nothing to solve; nothing to figure out.

When you wake from this sleep, you will feel refreshed. You'll feel like you've slept; your skin will feel brighter. Your thoughts will be clearer. You'll feel more patient and better able to deal with the challenges that come with the day. Your body will be stronger. Your muscles will have had time to heal from the stresses of carrying the weight and the exertions of life. Your digestive system will have had time to work, to reset, to carry nourishment to your organs and muscles, and to carry toxins away. The worries of today will be more manageable as your brain will have processed them, organize your thoughts.

This sleep will bring clarity and strength.

Bring the awareness now to your spine. Notice what happens to the spine as the breath enters and leaves your body. As you focus, you notice that with every inhale, the spine lengthens. It might be so subtle that you can barely feel it but keep awareness here for a moment. As the breath comes in, the spine lengthens. As the breath goes out, the spine relaxes.

Take a few breaths, and with each breath, notice this gentle, natural movement in the spine. The breath and the spine are always connected. The breath and the spine always support you.

 [Pause, 30 seconds]

Good.

There is twenty-four articulating vertebra in the spine. Bring the awareness now to the lumbar spine - the very bottom of the spine. Starting here, at the bottom, we'll slowly move the awareness up along the spine's length, one vertebra at a time. As you hear my voice mention each vertebra, imagine that the space between it and the one before it gets bigger. We are allowing the spine to relax fully.

So, starting at the bottom, in the lumbar spine:

Now moving to the thoracic spine - the middle section of the spine:

And then to the cervical spine, the top of the spine:

Bring the awareness to the whole of the length of the spine.

The spine is long. The spine is relaxed. The whole of the back is relaxed. The breath moves gently, naturally.

Beautiful. Take a few soft, easy breaths.

[Pause - one-minute soft breath/music]

The shoulders are soft. The legs are relaxed. The weight of the body is supported by whatever is beneath you; no effort in the body—nothing to do.

Notice the hands. The palms of the hands. The backs of the hands. The fingertips. Allow the hands to soften - no effort in the hands at all.

And then bring awareness to the face. Allow the jaw to soften - so there's just a little bit of space between the teeth. Allow the forehead to become smooth, releasing any worries that you hold there. And imagine that the whole of the head - the crown of the head, the back of the head - softens, relaxes, releases. Perhaps you feel the sensations of release; of letting go, just by noticing the head.

If any part of the body feels uncomfortable, adjust it now. Do any shuffling around that you need to do to feel completely comfortable? Make small - really small - movements with the head, side to side. You are allowing any tension left in the neck to gently, softly roll out. And then find stillness in the center when you're ready.

When you feel entirely, wonderfully, deeply comfortable, stay here. Enjoy this moment of utter comfort. Everything is as it should be. You are where you need to be. This perfect, soft, effortless comfort that you feel throughout the body is bliss. Your body will remember this feeling: the more you practice reaching this relaxed, effortless state, the easier it will be to get here. And you know that this is the perfect state to fall into a deep, happy sleep.

Keep breathing here gently.

[Pause; two minutes music]

The breath has a natural rhythm.

As you continue with this natural rhythm, making no effort to control it, repeat the following sentence silently to yourself:

"I am here. I am comfortable. I am calm."

Good. Repeat it to yourself twice more.

[Pause; 20 seconds music]

Bring the awareness, now, to the darkness behind the eyelids. Notice any colors that you see; any shapes or patterns that form in that deep, dark space. There's no need to try to decipher anything, here; just watch.

Now you are here. In the body. At this moment. Well done.

Start to imagine that you're lying underneath a beautiful tree. It's warm - the last sunlight of the day is touching your skin, that beautiful orange glow lighting up the sky, and dancing across the trees' leaves.

Notice the comfortable, warm temperature of your body. Notice the shape of the leaves on the tree; a warm breeze blows, and one of the leaves drifts lazily down to the ground. There's no one else around; this is your place—only yours. Notice the rise and fall of your abdomen as the breath keeps moving, easily, in and out. Your body is relaxed, and you are supported. The tree provides all the shelter you need.

Chapter 4: Vagus Nerve Stimulation and Stress Reduction Exercises

Yoga Self-Care

What makes a few of us ricochet back despite life's difficulties, and others disintegrate? Why is it that, a few days, we feel ready to take on the World, while on different days, one seemingly insignificant detail can set us off? There are, without a doubt, various responses to these inquiries be that as it may, on a physiological level, analysts realize that our pressure strength levels are associated with a certain something: the vagus nerve.

The vagus nerve, our tenth cranial nerve, adjusts the parasympathetic sensory system, the piece of the sensory system that causes us to quiet down and unwind. Likewise called the "meandering nerve" since it wanders through the body, the vagus nerve directs heart and breath rate and controls our voice tone, organs, and stomach related tract. From multiple points of view, the vagus nerve is the air traffic controller of our physical body—sending and getting messages from the cerebrum about when to process, when to inhale, and what to feel. This makes it a fundamental player in building pressure versatility.

Strangely, the condition of our vagus nerve can be estimated. Researchers built up a measure called pulse fluctuation, which tracks the time between heart pulsates. When there is changeability between heart thumps, this suggests a high vagal tone, which is associated with great pressure flexibility. When there is a little fluctuation between heart thumps, this suggests a low vagal tone, which is related to poor pressure versatility. The primary concern? When there is adaptability in our pulses, as opposed to an inflexible beating, we are stronger. Sounds entirely like yoga, isn't that so? Adaptability implies versatility and improved general wellbeing.

Fortunately, the vagus nerve can be reinforced through the way of life, practice, and aim. Here are a couple of practices that have been appeared to increment vagal tone.

Slow, Deep, Breathing

This training is, without a doubt probably the most ideal approaches to improve the quality of the vagus nerve. Researchers contend this is one motivation behind why yoga is so amazing—due to the accentuation on the breath. It encourages us to unwind by initiating the vagus nerve and supporting our sensory system. Have a go at delaying during work to inhale profoundly for a couple of seconds, and notice how you feel.

Exercise

Moderate to concentrated exercise has been appeared to improve pulse inconstancy, the marker of vagal tone. Studies show that normal exercise in sound grown-ups, just as grown-ups with cardiovascular illness, improved vagal tone. The exercise doesn't need to be long-only 20 minutes can have an effect. While look into this has not yet been done, it would appear to pursue that consolidating yogic breathing with moderate exercise would additionally upgrade the impacts of pressure versatility and vagal tone.

Metta Meditation

Metta reflection, otherwise called cherishing thoughtfulness contemplation, is simply the act of sending kind considerations to yourself as well as other people. Scientist Barbara Fredrickson found that Metta's contemplation improved vagal tone for some who rehearsed it. She contrasted a control bunch with those rehearsing Metta and found that when individuals revealed increments in warm and cherishing sentiments, their vagal tone improved. Have a go at rehearsing Metta contemplation as you nod off; not exclusively will you improve your vagal tone, you may likewise be emphatically affecting your fantasy life, as per the Buddhist writings.

Brief Recitation

An examination demonstrated that reciting om can improve vagal tone by invigorating the nerves around the throat. On the off chance that om isn't your thing, you can likewise have a go at singing noisily—what the hell, nobody's tuning in the vehicle. Feel the reverberation in your throat and all through your body.

Plainly yoga offers an assortment of apparatuses to increment vagal tone and along these lines, bolster pressure flexibility. The key is to rehearse at least one of these instruments every day, regardless of whether it's only for five minutes. Also, recall, it sets aside an effort to fortify the sensory system, yet persistence and practice can carry us to a progressively adjusted condition of being.

The vagus nerve is really a basket case driving from the gut through the heart and to the cerebrum. It's the longest cranial nerve and has correspondence with each organ.

Its fundamental capacity is to control the parasympathetic sensory system. The parasympathetic sensory system is a piece of the autonomic help framework known as the "rest and overview" framework. It assumes a job in pulse, sexual excitement, absorption, pee, and gastrointestinal action.

The vagus nerve works enthusiastically to control irritation. It alarms the cerebrum to discharge synapses when provocative proteins called cytokines are available. These synapses help the body fix at that point decrease aggravation.

Another capacity of the vagus nerve is to trigger the arrival of acetylcholine, which controls muscles, enlarges veins, and eases back pulse. It's sheltered to state the vagus nerve might be the most significant nerve that most of the individuals are as yet ignorant of.

Researchers have connected vagus nerve brokenness to heftiness, constant aggravation, wretchedness, uneasiness, seizures, unusually low pulse, blacking out, and GI issues.

Actually, the examination on this nerve has been promising to the point that vagus nerve triggers have been embedded in patients and discovered achievement even with untreatable sadness and epilepsy. The gadget is carefully embedded under the skin and sends an electrical sign to the vagus nerve. When invigorated, the vagus nerve begins speaking with the remainder of the body.

Fortunate for us, there's no requirement for medical procedures. Vagal tone can be improved normally through incitement with systems that should be possible at home. Attempting to reinforce your vagal tone will help with state of mind, processing, and general prosperity.

Nineteen efficient ways to Improve Vagal Tone

1. Swishing. This is presumably the least complex and most open route for an individual to chip away at their vagal tone. In the first part of the day, wash some water as hard as possible. You'll realize you've invigorated the vagus nerve when you start to get a tear reaction in your eyes.

2. Breathwork. Profound moderate breaths from the tummy will animate the vagus nerve. Sit or sit down and take in as much as you can. Hold it for a second or two and afterward discharge. Rehash this 5-10 times. You'll feel euphoric and lose a while later.

3. Giggling. Giggling discharges a huge amount of synapse, which improves vagal tone. Giggle hard and regularly.

4. Fish Oils. EPA and EHA lower pulse, which reinforces the vagal tone.

5. Fasting. The vagus nerve is the chief of the parasympathetic sensory system known as the rest and condensation framework. Offering the assimilation procedure, a reprieve through discontinuous fasting or fewer snacks for the duration of the day will likewise improve vagal tone.

6. Yoga. The breathing and development of yoga assist with absorption and has been appeared to build GABA levels. Improving GABA levels will animate the vagal tone.

7. Singing. Singing works the muscles in the back of the throat, which invigorates the vagus nerve. Simply make certain to sing as loud as possible for this impact to occur. An extraordinary spot to do this is in the vehicle.

8. Cold Showers. Cold showers are extreme from the start, yet they can enormously improve vagal tone. As you change in accordance with the cool, the thoughtful sensory system brings down, and the parasympathetic framework gets more grounded, legitimately influencing the vagus nerve.

9. Backrub. A back rub invigorates the lymphatics and improves the vagal tone.

10. Fragrance based treatment. Fundamental oils, for example, lavender and bergamot, have appeared to expand pulse inconstancy, which improves vagal tone.

11. Developing Positive Relationships

Research shows that just by thinking about our friends and family, we can tone and reinforce the vagus nerve, consequently receiving the numerous rewards that the nerve gives.

12. Presentation to the Cold

By drinking cold water or washing up, we reinforce our body's quieting framework (the parasympathetic framework), which occurs through the vagus nerve.

13. singing and Chanting

Singing as loud as possible expands pulse inconstancy and works the muscles in the back of your throat that associate with the vagus nerve.

14. Back rubs

Apart from feeling astounding, a great back rub of the feet and neck actives the vagus nerve and can diminish seizures.

15. Satisfaction and Laughter

Having a decent snicker lifts your mind-set, supports the insusceptible framework, and animates the vagus nerve.

16. Yoga and Tai Chi

Both Yoga and Tai Chi give a large group of medical advantages and are especially useful for those battling with wretchedness and nervousness.

17. Profound Breathing

Profound breathing animates the vagus nerve to bring down circulatory strain and pulse.

18. Exercise

Physical exercise is ground-breaking both for gut stream and psychological wellbeing benefits, which both happen by means of the vagus nerve.

19. Unwinding

Practically any loosening up action reinforces the vegas nerve's capacity to give recuperating to the body.

Therefore, these are ways that can help strengthen the vagal tone for you.

Chapter 5: College Sweethearts

When Carole and Jordon were freshmen in college, they met at a coffee cart outside of the main entrance to the old campus lot. Their meeting was like one straight out of a storybook, complete with cool fall weather, colorful leaves strewn about, and cozy scarves, and toques adorning everyone to help them stay warm. One morning in the fall of freshman year, Carole was standing with her friends in line at the coffee cart and Jordon was working the cart to earn some extra cash to help purchase new filming equipment. When Carole was next in line, she walked up to the cart and ordered an Americano with extra whip cream. "Odd order," Jordon answered, scribbling it down on a piece of paper. "Whip cream on coffee?" He asked. "Just the way I like it." Carole smiled, handing Jordon exact change for her drink. As she handed him the change, Carole and Jordon locked eyes and smiled, pausing for a moment to take in the simple and sweet beauty of falling in love with each other.

Carole thought Jordon was attractive, so she made a mental note of which cart he was working at and came back to that cart each morning for weeks after. Some mornings, Jordon would be working and he would prepare her drink for her. Others, he would not be working but he would always seem to be nearby the cart so that when she was done ordering they could share some conversation before they each parted way to attend their respective classes. Without ever telling the other, the two of them always did their best to ensure that they would see each other every single morning.

Carole and Jordon grew fond of their morning conversations. They also started getting braver and braver as they each began leaving little hints about having an attraction toward the other. Carole would always smile and give Jordon a hug if he was not working, and Jordon would always draw little smiley faces or hearts on Carole's Americano with the whipped cream. These two lovers had a great deal of fun falling for each other and enjoy casually flirting with one another each morning before classes.

One day, during the middle of winter, when it was particularly cold outside, Jordon proposed that the two of them head inside and grab a bite to eat. It just so happened that Carole did not have to be at class for another forty-five minutes, so she agreed and the two of them walked together to the cafeteria hall to eat their breakfasts with each other. They spent the entire time laughing, enjoying each other's company, and falling even more deeply in love with each other.

When the breakfast was done, the two parted ways and went to their respective classes. All morning, they both found themselves distracted by thoughts of the other. They loved how it felt so normal to be with each other, and how spending time together seemed to come so easily. When their classes were over that day, Carole went back to her dorm to study. At some point that evening, she heard a knock at her door. When she answered it, she saw none other than Jordon standing there, smiling, with his hands stuffed in his pockets. He paused for a moment before asking if she wanted to go to the library with him to study together, and Carole happily agreed. The two of them spent the evening studying, joking, and enjoying each other's company.

After that, Carole and Jordon began hanging out almost daily. They would share breakfast, study sessions, or even just walks around the campus as they enjoyed each other's presence. When spring break came, they carpooled back to see their family as they both came from the same small town in Connecticut. They would listen to their favorite songs on the ride back home, sing, laugh, and spend even more time getting to know each other along the way.

As the years went by, Carole and Jordon became inseparable. In sophomore year, they spent spring break on a vacation together in Cape Cod where they enjoyed delicious seafood dinners and beach walks together each evening. In junior year, they spent Christmas at each other's family's houses, enjoying two dinners, and sharing the opportunity to meet each other's extended families. By senior year, they fell so deeply in love that there was no way these two could be separated from each other's company.

When graduation was right around the corner, Jordon began acting strange. Carole thought he was reconsidering their relationship since college would be over soon and became worried that the love of her life was preparing to leave her. Jordon became scared because he had no idea what the love of his life would think about him wanting to spend the rest of their lives together. Shortly after the two walked across the stage, Jordon got down on one knee and proposed to Carole. He proposed that she marry him, that they move in together, that they start their careers, and that they eventually have the children and dogs that they always dreamed about having during their late-night study sessions. Carole cried as she realized that Jordon had been acting weird because he was about to propose, not because he was preparing to leave her. She said yes, and the two cried together as they celebrated the reality that they would go on to live the rest of their lives together. The two lived happily ever after, as they say in the fairy tales.

Chapter 6: The Peaceful Path

Gary was a forty-something-year-old man who had been working for the same office job for nearly twenty years now. He was a busy man with many meetings every day, bosses who had high expectations of him and a family at home who regularly demanded more of his time and attention than he felt he had to give. Gary always strived to be everything his family, boss, and friends wanted and needed him to be, yet he never felt like he could keep up. Often, he would find himself standing in the shower at the beginning of what would be a very long day attempting to wash away his troubling thoughts. Gary felt like his mind was racing all the time, and sometimes in the shower was his only opportunity to clear his thoughts so that he could feel at peace with himself. It never lasted, but for those few moments in the shower in between thoughts of what he had to get done that day he would feel fleeting sensations of relief.

One day, Gary went into work and it became too much for him to handle. He was already feeling guilty about missing his Mom's birthday dinner because of needing to be at work, so when his boss started yelling at him, Gary couldn't take it anymore. He found himself in the bathroom with the door locked, talking himself out of a panic attack, and trying to find a moment of peace. He realized this was happening more and more: he would become overwhelmed with the demands of life and be desperate to feel even a fleeting moment of peace in between the stress. Despite how hard he wished for it; Gary could never seem to find the peace that he was looking for.

Gary searched everywhere for the peace he desired. He tried buying the things that he believed would bring him peace, but all they did was cause him to feel sad when it didn't work. He tried to create peace by purchasing expensive vacation packages for his family, but all he felt was stressed over the added expenses that he had to incur. He tried to talk to local yogis and meditation guides to try and find out how to get peace into his life, and while he understood the logic behind all of their teachings, Gary would not allow himself to actually do what the guides said. Instead, he would write off their suggestions as being "too easy" and then he would begin going about his life as usual.

Gary spent years upon years trying to find out how he could find peace, and eventually, he gave up. He became so fed up that the methods he was trying were not working that he decided peace must be an illusion and that everyone claiming to have it must be lying. Gary became so angry with all of the yogis and meditation guides in his town that any time he heard someone talk about them he would frown, claim that peace was a load of nonsense and that it was unattainable, and then end the conversation or leave.

One day, Gary became so angry with his failure to find peace and his deep-seated need for experiencing peace, that he threw his hands up in the air and admitted defeat. He was in his car after work, sitting in the grocery parking lot, and he was truly angry after being cussed out by his boss for the duration of the day. To put it simply, Gary was fed up with his life and he had reached the point where he could no longer take it. With his hands in the air, Gary yelled at the skies out of the front window of his car. "I can't take it anymore!" He shouted, dropping his fists into his lap and leaning his head over the steering wheel. "I can't take the stress, the demands, the overwhelm. I love my family and I can't even handle them anymore! It's too much!" He muttered, feeling his eyes flooding hot with tears. Now, this was a big deal for Gary. Gary was a very proud man, he was so proud that he rarely showed his anxiety, stress, or anger to anyone else. So, for Gary to be sobbing out all of his pent-up stress in his car was a big deal.

 After several minutes of sobbing in his car and releasing the stress that he had been carrying around inside of him, Gary found that there were no tears left. Almost suddenly, he no longer had the fear of what he had been holding on inside of him anymore, there was no sadness or stress left to be experienced in that moment. Gary sat up, wiped his eyes, and looked around his car to make sure that no one had seen him lose it in the grocery store parking lot. When he realized he was alone, and that all of his emotions had been felt, Gary felt a surge of peace rush through him. Just like that, he found what he had been looking for all along. In that moment, Gary realized that peace was not something that he could buy, manufacture, or obtain. Instead, peace was an emotion like any other, and it could be experienced and expressed through allowing himself to just be.

From that day forward, Gary made a routine of allowing himself private space to feel and express his emotions to himself. This way, he could continue to hold his pride around his family, without carrying the burden of his stress with him, too. As a result, Gary became a happier, healthier, and more peaceful man overall. He even joined a few of those meditation classes and followed some local yogi's through their practices as he learned to cultivate even more peace from within.

Chapter 7: A Day at the Beach

Before we begin this journey downwards into the deepest realms of our sub-conscious, let us take a minute to physically and mentally and spiritually acclimate ourselves into being with awareness of our inner-sanctum, our internal workings. We will begin by going to a place of comfort, ideally a bed, or a very comfortable reclining chair, and we will relax our bodies to the furthest extent possible. Now, close your eyes, staying firmly on your back, with your arms relaxed at your sides and your legs rested downwards. Take one deep breath in, through your nostrils, counting slowly to four, and one deep breath out, through your nostrils again, counting slowly to four. Breathe in the breath of the spirit and breathe out the stress of the day. Now is the time to rest. Become aware of nothing but the air flowing through your nostrils, envision a steady flowing stream, smooth inhalations and exhalations, your body become weightier and more relaxed with each passing cycle of breath. Allow your thoughts to become completely still, as you focus on your core, your solar plexus, allowing your thoughts to flow outwards past your vision until they escape your being, while only holding and retaining the pure awareness of spirit, the holy serenity of the mind and body. Breathe in, one, two, three, four, then breathe out, one, two, three, four, each breath becoming slower. One... two... three... four... One... two... three... four... One... two... three... four... One... two... three... four... One... two... three... four... One... two... three... four... Continue this pattern of breath, expanding, and sink down deeper into yourself, becoming a voyeur of your own still, relaxed body, lost in time. Become lost in this experience as you journey further into the trance, and prepare for the road we are about to embark upon. Draw further and further away from your still, lying body, and into the realm of imagination, where images grow, the land of dreams that you are about to become one with. Erase your mind of all that is within it currently, and prepare the landscape for a new and fresh experience, in the farther reaches of reality. One... two... three... four... inhale... One... two... three... four... exhale... One... two... three... four... inhale... One... two... three... four... exhale... Now, with your mind, body, and spirit rested totally, entranced, and fertile, let us begin.

You have taken a day off to spend at the beach. You are alone, and feel totally comfortable in your own skin. Around you are large crowds, but they feel very far away from you, and their presence does not overwhelm you in the slightest. There is a bubble around you, and, in fact, the presence of the crowd is uplifting, both in its juxtaposition with yourself, and in its own self-sustainability. These crowds of people are happy and loving and having the greatest times of their lives, and they are totally independent of you, and need nothing from you, as you need nothing from them. There is a great peace in this that you feel, a calm that there could be so much right in the World that exists totally without any need from you. It is inspiring and uplifting, and makes you feel free. The presence of the crowds does absolutely nothing to affect your ability to enjoy the natural pleasures of the beach. It seems as if the crowd has parted perfectly to allow you the best view possible of the shore and the horizon. You wonder how far out the water is visible. It could be one mile, or a hundred. To you, what you are seeing seems infinite, and infinitely calm. You feel as if you could walk across the beach and into the water and drift forever into the void of this great blue mass, and there would be no end in sight. At the edge of what is visible to you, the sky opens up, being an even greater and holier chasm, the abyss of the sea spread exponentially into the universe. It is amazing to you to watch these two divine forces, reflections of each other, connect and touch and embrace. It is you, yourself, embracing the infinite. The sand around you, likewise, is infinite, being an infinite number of grains. Every handful that you pick up and allow to pass through your fingers is infinity, a universe of universes. You are humbled by the sheer number of particles that make up this small space within your bubble, and in it's close proximity your mind wanders exponentially to the infinities lying elsewhere, within the other infinities, the small, personal spaces that make up our existence, and the endless number of spaces there can be. You are melting into the ground through your beach towel, as every particle of you intermingles with the endless particles in the sand, and every particle in your soul floats into the breeze towards the shore, interspersing through the waters until they end their journey at the horizon, at which point the dust will float up through the heavens, and eternity. You are melting, sinking, and your mind is leaving your body. Time slows down inside of your bubble as it speeds up among those crowds that had once been around you, now light-years away. Generations come and go among the beach crowds, as you remain perfectly still, and content, a part of something greater than yourself, yet which is only great because of yourself, the infinity. An eternity passes and you are back on the beach. You get up, the beach air bringing new life back into your lungs, and your blood, and your body, and your mind. Your eyes gaze anew upon the sight as you make your way towards the water, through the path that has been cleared by the universe through this large, intangible crowd that seems totally unaware of your presence. It is an infinite and joyous walk to the shore, and feels like walking towards the light, towards the afterlife. You feel the sand become wet at your feet, and where the particles once brushed up into the crevices of your feet and fell through, now they are molding into you, a larger mass, bonded by the water, each step leaving an impression in the sand which welcomes you with open arms, like a slipper that fits just right. Eventually, your feet feel the total submersion into the water, and the sand totally beneath. Instantly, you are connected most tangibly to the entire whole. Whereas you were always a part of this abyss, now it has awakened within you tenfold, and upon first touch you feel the water connecting to the sky at the horizon, connecting to the heavens above. There is only blue, a great, blue abyss, a serenity that perpetuates outwards for eternity. You continue, and continue to be submerged. As the water goes up above your waistline, you feel your entire body become weightless. You look back and see the crowds, and it feels as if you are in space looking back down onto the planet from which you came. In a beautiful way, the people on the beach seem like insects, and you feel totally removed from any part of them. The void behind you is what you feel the closest kinship with; it's infinite stretches and unending silence and space. You fall back into the water, and as it touches your head your mind melts away into this endless sea of blue. You are now flowing, totally weightless, into the abyss. You float for what seems like hours, then days, then weeks, then months, then years, then a lifetime, then further generations down, but it is only a second. This continues for a long while before you have reached that horizon, that point that you saw back on the beach where the blue of the waters transcended into the blue of the sky. With this meeting, you transcend as well, as your entire being transmutes into the air, becoming the glowing golden clouds of the sunset. You are as large as the entire visible sky, looking down at the place you came from, glowing golden between the earth and the heavens. For an eternity, the sun sits at the horizon, projecting you onto the clouds, the golden glow of your soul. As it fades, your consciousness fades, and the whole of your golden glow becomes broken into infinite pieces, becoming the multitude of stars in the sky. Now you are in space, divided amongst the cosmos, neither here nor there, in infinite black. You are totally still, you are the night sky, and you are asleep.

Chapter 8: The Hare Pirates on A Treasure Hunt

It is a beautiful day. There is not a single cloud in the sky far and wide. On the shallow water a pirate ship crosses across the sea.

The sun shines on the sailor. But there is no time for laze. On the ship is once again looking diligently for a treasure island. Because the pirate's thirst for gold and jewels.

The helmsman still does not know exactly where the journey should go. Because so far, the pirates sail only on the basis of a half treasure map. To find the treasure, you must first look for the other half of the treasure map.

But now there is another problem for now. At the stern of the ship an octopus has settled. That slows down the whole ride. The captain takes a short piece of wood and heads for the octopus. Then he throws the wood as far as he can into the sea. He calls out loud and the octopus jumps from the stern into the water and swims behind the stick. "Well, then you go water-terrier!" The captain whispers in his beard before he goes back to the treasure hunt.

And there it sounds already from the lookout tower: "Land ahead! Hard port! "The captain pushes the helmsman aside and tears the helm around with a grin. In front of them an island appears on the horizon. Is this the treasure island? Hard to say without the second part of the map. But it's a start. Hustle is spreading on the pirate ship. The sails are reset quickly. Every hare on board hurries as best he can. Why the rabbits are so hectic you ask?

Well, they are not the only ones looking for the treasure. Other pirates have sneaked the first part of the treasure map and are now looking for wealth and honor.

One evening, the captain's right paw - the lanky Hellgard Hüpfer - was not paying close attention and fell asleep while the treasure map was lying on his bedside table. This moment was maliciously exploited. A devious pirate sneaked into the sleeping chamber of the captain's right paw to secretly draw the treasure map. And now the pirates are in competition with the insidious villains. First come first serve.

True, the Pirates Code does not prohibit treacherously providing an advantage; but he commands the one who finds him first.

The island is getting closer and the lookout is getting loud. "Second part of the treasure map ahead!" Willi gets far-sighted and falls from sheer excitement almost from the observation deck. Phew, that just went well.

When the captain hears the call, he does not trust his eavesdroppers. He rushes to the railing of the pirate ship and reaches for the telescope. "Where? Where? "He exclaims excitedly. But then he sees something that makes his blood freeze in his veins.

The second part of the treasure map is in a bottle post. But this was already fished out of the sea. The captain sees the unbelievable in the distance. "Ai Potz flash. Someone fries an Easter egg for me. This is a Meerjungzibbe holds the Boddel. "Poltert it from the nose of the captain.

And indeed. On the island sits a mermaid, er, sorry, baby boy - as the captain already said - and holds the message in his paws.

There is caution. Because, as the captain already really rumbles on: "With Meerjungzibben is not just cherries eat mi Jung!"

And he orders the sailor to catch up with the sails and slow down.

Then he roars with all his might: "Guns starboard!" All sailors hurry frantically. Then the cannons are dragged to starboard. The sailors sing in rhythm: "And one and draw and one and move ..."

The ship swings from left to right, from right to left. It rocks so hard that some cannons roll back by themselves. "Ai pats again! Just stay a while! "Cries the young Torben dub, as he is pulled by a cannon across the deck.

With all his might he tries to hold the monster. But there is nothing to do. The cannon continues indefatigably on its way. To make matters worse, he stumbles over a plank and flies in a high arc on the rolling cannon.

Now both of them dash past the other pirates with Karacho. Two sailors can take cover at the last moment before the cannon with a bang and the poor Torben dub with a dull - PATSCH - crash against the gang of the ship.

The other sailors can hardly keep from laughing. "That was a clean crash landing, mi Jung! These are cannons and not horses! "The laughter breaks out of the thick pirate Kunjard sausage.

"Well wait," thinks Torben dub and gets up. When he has the cannon back in the right place he deliberately jumps on the tube as if he wants to ride the monster. Then he grabs the fuse, lights the fire and gets ready.

When all the cannons are aligned, the ship is close enough to the island to deliver the first salvo. Now the other pirates ignite the blazing fire and get ready.

"Fire free!" Thundered the captain's powerful voice over the planks. The Lunten are ignited and with a deafening roar hurl the cannon balls from the steel pipes into the open air.

The cannons bounce a bit backwards. Torben dumbs up an arm and yells, "Jiiihah." Sitting on the cannon like a cowboy doing a rodeo.

The other sailors and pirates marvel not bad at the daring pirate boys. Especially not when they see Torben's butt caught fire. Everyone looks at him with big eyes.

Torben himself does not notice and sits proudly like Oskar on the cannon. "N / A? You did not think so, did you? "He boasts. But then he perceives the smell of burnt fur.

He sniffs and sniffs - looks around - and keeps sniffing. "What is it that offends my sense of smell?" He asks when suddenly he discovers the fire on his bottom.

He jumps frantically into the next water barrel. After a loud "Splash Pfffffffff" you can only see steam rising. Soaking wet, the poor dork sits in the barrel. And everyone can laugh heartily again.

In the meantime, the mermaid has heard the tremendous bang and jumped in the water. The bottle post with the second part of the treasure map has dropped her.

When the pirate Marla Mutig saw this, she jumped boldly over the plank to get the Boddel. Now she is also spotted by the lookout. "Hare overboard!" Calls Willi Weitsicht just when he suddenly notices that one of the insidious treasure maps thieves' sneaks over the main sail.

Down on deck, meanwhile, a large piece of wood is flying past the captain's head. Amazed, he turns around and sees the octopus from earlier. Apparently, she has found the stick and wants the captain to throw it again.

Meanwhile, standing on the mast now the rogue with drawn saber directly in front of Willi Weitsicht and mumbled: "I make you shish kebab on the spit." But there it rang from the deck: "Sails clear her water rats!" Bellowed the captain.

He had long since noticed the other pirate ship and does not hesitate to fire long. Immediately the sailors clear the sails and the attacker is swept off the main mast like spinach from the kitchen table. The rogue lands in the sea with a belly slapper.

The octopus jumps happily afterwards. She probably thinks the villain is a stick. You do not want to get stuck in his skin now. It only takes a moment and the rogue flies screaming over the pirate ship. The octopus thought it was too good with the momentum.

After the rogue has flown past the captain, he grabs the telescope and searches in the distance for Marla Mutig in the water. He cannot find her.

"Marla come on - where are you? A water rat like you is not drowned, "he whispers to himself. The captain knows they have to hurry if they want to find the treasure first. And there Marla Mutig is his best chance.

The captain cannot find the pirate in the water at all. For now, she has collected the bottle post and has swum to the island. She just wants to open the message in the bottle when she sees it.

Just within reach, suddenly everything seems in vain. The second part of the map is no longer legible. The mermaid had opened the message in the bottle before leaping into the water. Now the treasure map is saturated with salt water. All the ink has gone and the treasure seems lost.

Marla stares at the card and falls to her knees. Was everything else now? The salt water on the treasure map is now joined by Marla's tears. She is sobbing and crying. Should everything really be over now?

But as luck would have it, there is a happy ending. Because when Marla looks up, she sees the treasure chest standing right in front of her. The mermaid had already found the treasure. She sat on it just before, without the pirate noticing.

Marla Mutig wipes away her tears and retrieves the golden key from the bottle. Then she puts him in the lock of the chest - the key fits. With a "crack" the lock opens. That's the end of the race - because the Pirate Code rules, who found it first, can keep it.

The captain has now also spotted Marla Mutig and the treasure on the island and shouts to the crew: "We have found the treasure! Today there are carrots for everyone and in abundance! "The pirates jump joyfully up and down.

The insidious villains, however, do not look very happy. According to the Pirate Codex, you lost the race for the treasure. And so, they leave untapped things and no prey.

Marla has meanwhile ransacked the treasure chest. The box contains bags of gold, jewelery and jewelery. Most notable, however, is a ring with a diamond twice as large as Marla's paw.

When the other pirates finally reach the island, the joy is still great! It is cheered and celebrated until the sun goes down. Once again, a treasure was found. Only the ring with the big diamond has disappeared. Well, who has that?

Chapter 9: The Dream Life

Just when you think life cannot get any worse than it currently is, either something magical can happen that will change your luck or it gets a little bit worse. Those are the only two options, after today you wonder how your luck will go, will it better? Or will your life come crashing down around you? You hear a knock on the door, your tired body drags you to answer it. You open the door to see a business woman, smiling largely as she hands you a heavy briefcase. Puzzled you don't want her to release the case. Who is this woman? Why is she here? Your brain struggles to process this, then she starts talking.

"You are the winner of the dream life sweepstake. You are the luckiest person on Earth right now, and everything is going to change for the better." This feels like a gimmick, surely, she will say you only need to invest, blah, blah, blah. So, you tell her that you are not interested and you just want her to leave you in peace so you can rest. She is dumfounded as you shut the door in her face.

As you walk back to your bed, your phone rings. You answer it to hear a formal voice on the other line announce that he's a lawyer for the World's richest man, a man who died a few weeks ago. In his will he had a list of names, people that he had encountered in his life...everyone from the school librarian in primary school to a drive thru window cashier at the McDonald's. Anyone he met, he added them to this list. Upon his death he wanted his list to become a sweepstakes for his fortune, but his money ruined his life. It tore apart his family, it made him greedy, it made him lazy. He wants someone to be able to live out their dream life, through his will, but with guidance. The lady at the door is the first step towards guiding you to accepting this fortune. After the lawyer explains, you still can't seem to process this. You don't think you met this man, and if you had...would you be so lucky as to win his entire fortune?

Is this that point where your luck changes? Will it be the best thing that ever happened to you? Or will you waste your time? Isn't it worth the amount of time, just to listen to the lady? What harm can it do? You turn around and walk back to the door. Allowing the woman to enter your home. You have a seat at the table and she opens the brief case. "First, we will start with a questionnaire. I am to guide you to a dream life, not just hand you a fortune. Once that I am certain you are ready to have the fortune, it will be all yours." You hesitantly agree, still feeling this is too good to be true.

What is your dream job, do you wish to earn fulfillment through your work, or is it a means to an end? You decide you have nothing to hide from this woman, so you tell her the truth. She nods and moves on to the next question.

What is your dream family? Do you have it? Would money change your family, for the better or for the worse?

If you could live anywhere in the World, where would you live? Why would you live there?

"Ok, that takes care of the basics. Give me a few moments and I'll be back soon." As she leaves the room, you suddenly find yourself a bundle of nerves. Your body is tense and achy. You want to relax yourself, not let this work you up. So, you take a deep breath in as you stretch and flex the muscles in your body. As you exhale slowly, you allow the muscles to relax. You can feel a warm tingling sensation rushing through as you repeat the process. You keep breathing in slowly, becoming aware of your body. It is heavy and tired; you relax into the chair and focus on the simple task of breathing and allowing your body to rest. The lady enters the room again and you feel relaxed, maybe this is for the best. "Now, we will start building your dream life. Starting with some major purchases, then working through the minor ones so we can organize your new life. What type of car do you wish to have? Do you need anything custom on it?" She hands you a form, as you order your dream car.

You think about all the cars you've wanted throughout your life, until you finally settle on one. You try to keep in mind, this is because you're not spending your own money. This is just a 'dream' car for a reason. Think of every elaborate detail you would want in that car, including a personal driver, if that's what you want. Once you have etched every detail into that paper, hand it back to her.

"Now, we can decide on your land. I got some listings in the areas you described as your dream location. Please, look over these and see if any of them are what you had in mind."

As you look through the real estate listings, you see so many perfect opportunities. They are exactly where you would want to build a dream home. You look at the surrounding areas and you can picture the beautiful landscape now. Hearing the local noises. Smelling the scents, feeling the peace it would bring to you to be there now. You realize you've held onto this particular listing for a while. You let her know this is the one you like the most. Her fingers fly across her phone as she informs you that the land now belongs to you. All the paperwork will be signed at the end. You are dumbfounded as you look at her and ask, "Why me? How did I know this man, why would he want to give me this dream life?"

"I don't know the details. I just know that your name was on his list, and it is the name that was selected. My job is planned out in exquisite details, which is why we are able to shuffle along through these tasks. You are in fact a very lucky person, with a great fortune. Let's not lose momentum now, the sooner we have everything in order, the sooner you get to experience your dream life. The best contractor and his team are prepared to draw up your dream house when you are ready. They will be here shortly, I have just sent them the land, so they will have a better idea on how to make things work for you. While we wait for them, are you happy in your current dwellings? Or do you want a new temporary home while your dream home is being constructed?"

You think long and hard on the question. Now that money is apparently not a problem, what do you want to do while your dream home is being constructed? Do you want to live here and just wait? Do you want to hire movers and move into a nice upscale place? Or a place far away from everyone and everything while you process your new life? Surely, you'll want to escape the media, if you stay in your current dwellings, you need people to help keep the media off you. Or maybe you'll step into the spot light and shine, embracing your dream life. When you thought of what you wanted you let the lady know and she assures you that nothing will be a problem. All your wishes for your new life will be answered.

The contractor has arrived with his team, only now that it is not just this lady in front of you, or the voice on the phone from earlier, the reality is really sinking in. Your life is going to become everything you've ever wanted. As they bring in their things and get settled you start to wonder what you will do with your life?

With all your worries fading quicker and quicker into your past, what does your soul want? When everything material in this World becomes easily bought, what are the things you need to work on? How can you be the person that you truly want to be? Do you need all this money to accomplish your goals? Will it make your life that much easier? Probably, but when all those little inconveniences are covered, and no longer troublesome, does your life feel empty or is there a vast opening that you can now explore? Will you travel the World? Will you fund new charities or help those already established?

The contractor introduces himself and starts to ask questions about your dream home so that they may begin the process...you feel your mind flood with images of beautiful houses, but you don't know where to start. You inhale and exhale and decide right now to start becoming the new you, as you describe this home. This home reflects who you are as a person. Build it from the ground up. Describe how you want your base, in detail, build your dream home, until you drift into a deep peaceful rest. When you wake up tomorrow, you will be this new person with a strong base to work on your dream life.

Chapter 10: The Secret Cabin

You have just left your car in the safe lot behind you. You walk upon the woods from the graveled lot, as you make your way onto the path you stop to admire the beauty. You close your eyes as you look up through the autumn leaves. Feeling the sunlight warm your face and smelling the crispness of the turned leaves. As the sun light dances behind your eyelids you feel yourself calm and relax, ready to journey through this forest of warm sunshine and mellow color. Opening your eyes as you lower you head back you take in all the richness around you. Many of the trees full with vibrant colors, some are evergreen, and some are showing their branches as their shaken off the old and are ready to embrace the new. You haven't explored this forest before, but you are going to meet a friend in a cozy cabin that is deep in the forest.

This small get away and escape from our technical World is exactly what you need. Taking a deep breath, you start to wander down the well-worn foot path. The path welcoming you as it has many strangers in the past. As you walk the leaves giving a slight, satisfying crunch as your comfy hiking shoes cradle your feet. The once lush forest is in preparation for the upcoming winter. Just like your body settles in for the rest, it must prepare. As you feel your body settling in to the autumnal shifts you notice the squirrels scurrying about, collecting their supply for their own long rest. The birds have mostly headed south and the only noise you can hear is the slight rustle of the leaves as a crisp wind blows through.

As you keep exploring into the woods, you come up on a large pine tree. You stop to briefly admire it, and you are amazed by the sheer size of it. This is the biggest tree you have ever seen. You cannot even see the very top, just lush and thick, deep green branches all the way to the top. You wonder how long this tree has been here. The things it must have been around to experience. Perhaps this tree was only a tiny sapling when your great, great ancestors were establishing the family that would eventually lead to you. Of all the cosmic events and paths of mother nature, one has led to you. Just like the many stages in your life they all have a beginning and an ending.

Nature is pleasantly predictable as all things follow a natural order, the sun rises, the sun sets, and a new day comes. You must rest in between to have a long, healthy life. This seed was planted. With nourishment it began to grow. Despite all odds, life continues. Saplings are able to grow into gigantic pine trees. You feel that slight breeze as it blows through and ruffles your hair, reminding you that you need to reach the cabin. You continue on the footpath... further from the city, closer to the still calmness of forest. The sounds of the city and busy roads are far behind you now. A distant memory as your body adjusts to the new sounds in the forest. Your body openly accepts the welcoming relaxation that the World is providing.

Your eyes relax with the warm colors surrounding you, the deep amber, the golden yellows, and the harvest orange of the leaves. You meander through the wooded land and you notice a new sound. A pleasant sound of the faintest trickle of a babbling brook. As you travel closer to the brook you can see the stream flowing smooth and calm, causing the smallest of waterfalls as the water caresses the round rocks. There is a striking green moss around the stream causing an ethereal appearance to this mystical place. The stream, clear and meandering feels fresh, like it could wash away all your troubles just by being near it. Let the stream carry away any thoughts that are hindering you. Toss them into the stream and they can be washed away for another time. You watch your troubles slip away on the surface of the stream and you start to walk along beside the water.

As the stream wraps around the path you see a small wooden bridge arcing over the pathway. Weather worn but sturdy the bridge gives a little sigh as you walk across it. Holding on to the handrail you can feel the warmth from the sun radiating through your body. Though all this land is new for you, it oddly feels like coming home. Like the surrounding warmth you feel around you is familiar. It welcomes you with open arms and you wonder how much longer until you'll reach the cabin, how wonderful will it be? A little up ahead you can see a split in the path, as you get closer you can read the hand carved sign pointing to the right. Nightingale cabin is very close. Only a short distance to travel and you'll be ready for your vacation of peace and relaxation. The dense forest starts to give way to bigger rocks, hinting that you have explored yourself further to edge of the mountain. To the left you can see as the vegetation has thinned out to make way for mountain cliffs, you will explore those later. For now, you just want to settle in.

Your pack starts to feel heavy on you. As if it has been weighing your body down with every step. Your legs long to rest, but you know there is not much further to go. Up ahead on the horizon you see the cabin. The green tin roof stands out against the autumn colors surrounding it. The welcoming warm woods and white trim make this cabin appear to be cozier than its grand scale depicts. The round logs only giving way to grand white framed windows. Your tiredness turns into relief as you walk up the three short stairs to the welcoming door. Seeing a note on the door you read that your friend has went out briefly but will return in a while. In the meantime, you are instructed to make yourself at home. You turn the knob and open the door, as you move through the threshold there is one sight that captivates you.

The large sightseeing windows provide a picturesque mountain overlook as you can now see the cabin is perched near a cliff. The colorful trees, spotted with occasional evergreens is breath taking. You focus on your breathing as you look among the trees, breathing in, then slowly releasing that breath. How many different colors can you see? Breathing in you count 1, 2, 3. Breathing out you count more. Do this until you've discovered all the colors there are to be seen in this beautiful forest that surrounds you. This welcoming home away from home.

You take off your pack and notice the kitchenette is to the left, the rooms off to the right, but directly ahead of you in front of the welcoming windows is a great room. You set your pack on the table by the entrance for now. You'll settle in your things later. Now it is time to rest your body. The great room has a fire place with wood and kindling ready to go, you notice the slight chill in the air so you decide starting a small fire is a good idea. You take the small logs from the top of the pile, along with some kindling, and place them into the fire place. You notice the matches on a coffee table behind you and you use them to light this fire. As the small fire blossoms to life with a small roar and crackles you can feel the heat drifting off it. Feeling the warmth makes you realize there is a slight coldness that has seeped in from walking through the autumn forest. You look around the great room. Seeing the warm colors in the cabin reflecting those that are all around you in the woods.

There is an inviting brown leather sofa in the center of the room, with a deep red throw. You lie down on the sofa and sink down further into the comfort, pulling the throw around you and banishing all cold from your body. The warmth surrounding you as you hear the slight crackle of the fire. A light rain has started out side and you can hear the pitter patter on the green tin roof as you see the cold rain falling outside you are grateful to be inside. Warm and cozy, with softness snuggled all around you. As you close your eyes again you can feel the warm colors comforting your senses. The cabin is quiet, your mind is relaxed, your body finally relaxes fully. Letting your arms down to your fingers drift off to sleep. Your neck and all down your spine, sinks into the sofa, relaxing on the most comfortable surface. Your legs all the way down to your toes sink further down off to sleep. You mind drifts of to relax with the rest of your body. Let it relax, there is nothing holding you back. Your vacation starts now, your only job is to let everything slip away as your mind embraces the nothingness that is complete peace.

Chapter 11: Night dream

"If you are that worn outside, then head to bed," mum said. And that I really did, even though Darkness did not come back yet out my window. My arms were so weak I could not get off my socks. They kept sticking with my toes. I crawled under the covers. When I am very exhausted, I fantasy......that I must visit the bank for some cash. Dad's birthday is tomorrow. And I would like to buy him something super-duper unique.

"Hurry," mother said, "until` the bank closes" She constantly reminds me I've My own cash. Occasionally I overlook my bankbook states I have $36 bucks left. The bus driver is quite fine when I inform him, I don't have any cash. "However, I will pay you back once I get some in the lender," I state.

We journey down busy roads, beyond tall buildings and I leap off the three Steps in the bus. There's a very long line of folks in the bank. Along with also the Teller's wicket seems like it's a mile off. So I rely bushels of butterflies while awaiting. Ultimately it is my turn. And I appear at this guy behind the countertop.

He has to be eight feet tall. Initially I thought that he was really wonderful.

"There is no money here for you," he explained. "You should have spent it all."

"But...however, my mom said there is a few lefts," I replied. "I stored it all Myself from my newspaper route."

"Then you must check with her," said the man sternly. "Or you have to 've arrived at the wrong lender," he explained, displaying his teeth.

I looked to his eyes again. And watched his grin. Was he faking for a sly coyote? Last summer, I found you at a field near my property. The creature appeared doomed with his hairy tail.

On the way home I met a great woman. When I informed her sad story, " she sensed Sorry for me. She should have been wealthy because she gave me an entire bag full of cash. I could not take all of it. I gave her rear a pile of paper cash. If she had to purchase a bag of fries, or visit a picture.

I do not need to move home. I've got enough cash for an Amazing present for My dad. "Something very unique," I mention into a white bunny, sitting on the chair beside me. I believe he's after me home.

"You're careful, the coyote does not attempt to consume you," I state. I show him teeth. However, it does not frighten him.

Around the corner, there's a small girl standing on the pavement. I get Off the bus to determine why she's crying. "My hands are cold," she explained. I bought her a pair of red mittens. She's so amazed she dared to thank me personally.

Now I'm hungry, and exhausted. I sit down on the sidewalk and start my Birthday present knapsack. There's half an apple sliced sandwich, and 2 chocolate chip cookies. Shortly my knapsack is vacant, except for a single crust. It attempts to hide from the corner.

"If I had a blueberry jam," I told the bus driver awaiting me. "It could be yummy with this crust of bread"

"I will take you to where blueberries are big. And succulent," he explained.

The bus brought me away in town, and over a crowded highway. Even beyond Fishing boats at the harbor.

Subsequently the bus turned up a gravel street. I observed a pheasant hurry throughout the street. We moved beyond fields of hay along with a large mountain, and we eventually ceased. The bus had a flat tire.

I got off and appeared a valley full of blueberries. And awaiting Beside the very first bush was the white bunny. "How can he find me?" I wondered.

I immediately filled my knapsack with succulent berries. My palms look like they are painted blue. And that my back is tired of bending over a lot. I sat on a log and also removed my shoe and sock. Then I started to shout. I had been fearful the coyote could return and bite my fur.

What exactly was I doing here? I believed. There aren't any presents for daddy. Besides, that sly coyote may find me. After conducting just like thunder throughout a subject I tripped over a log. Then fell to a tiny creek, using squishy mud. Was something pursuing me? Perhaps it was white bunny. I shook myself tender, how my friend's pet does. Spotty is his title. I mean that is the puppy's name. I discovered more yelling.

However, it seemed far off. My eyes were shut tightly. The same as the front door once I slam it.

...Subsequently I open my eyes one at a time. Mother and dad are looking at me. The kitty is on my bed. And I am too. While I look from the window, then the coyote's face is not there. And He's laughing. I chased my mom. She starts to laugh also. Oh...Oh. I forgot to Get Dad's current. Close my eyes I rush back to my own dreaming.

Chapter 12: A Bedtime Story for Adults

Once on a time in a far-off Location far away from Whatever there Dwelt a Boy and a woman.

No.

That is an adult story.

Once on a time in a far-off location, away from whatever, there dwelt a Man and a girl. His name was Johann and hers had been Elise. Johann had white skin and Elise's has been brownish. This did not matter at the beginning, but over the years, it might, initially in tiny ways, little cracks, then in ways they might no more ignore. Johann first found Elise at a smoke-filled area, and decided he wanted her, desired to understand the flavor of her brown skin, then desired to run his hands on the soft curves of her body. Elise did not consider him. Elise allow him have a drink in her home because she had been lonely. She allowed him touch her since she had been another sort of starving. She put with him enjoyed the meat of the own body against hers, the way his tough hands held her how his lips brushed her buttocks. Johann brought her joy and she brought him joy and afterwards, he put next to her, even breathing deep. Elise thanked him. She advised him to depart. He did but pledged to come back, ignoring her protests.

Johann delivered Elise a gorgeous aroma of fragrant wildflowers. She predicted and thank you and don't do this but she places the flowers on the coffee table in her living room and then smiled at them daily. He chose to call and occasionally she replied and they spoke about all types of items. Johann whined in his pursuit along with Elise finally reverted and followed him to dinners and from time to time, they'd drinks and occasionally they saw moving images and that she always let him spend the evening. Shortly, Elise had abandoned there was a moment when she did not desire Johann around.

The guy was so distinct. Elise frequently worried that he was too distinct. Johann Worked with his palms and hadn't been outside the boundaries of this far away location far out of anything. He understood things about the celebrities and the job of sunlight. He understood about key waterfalls in the core of the deep forests and then he showed them to her, then allow her drink that cool fresh water out of his rough, calloused hands-on. Elise worked together with her head and occasionally her heart. She understood about words spent days studying novels. She spoke different languages and had traveled into lands across seas and farther even. She longed to become nearer to areas where she might discover bright lights and busy roads and at which at a while, she would see somebody who looked just like her. However, Elise had a project to perform and research to finish. She'd bide her time. Johann and Elise knew little of the very same items but he knew just how to get and the way to push his lips on her throat and the way to maintain her because she slept and when all that mattered was that the minutes shared between them all, they all might have easily discovered a happily ever afterwards.

There were, but other things. Johann had a wicked mum Who dwelt in a grand home high on a mountain. She maintained a lush backyard and appreciated getting visitors at a sizable living room full of big, imposing furniture. The wicked mother scowled over she awakened. The wicked mother believed her son that a king and desired nothing but the very best for her oldest boy. She didn't believe Elise was some other sort of great and she let this be known across the property. Elise attracted Johann's wicked mommy presents and kind words. She said please and thank you when invited to supper, she made to wash dishes. Not one of her expressions could influence the wicked mom who didn't desire Johann to enjoy a girl with this kind of distinct skin. It was a scandal, " she explained. Consider the household, " she explained. Shortly, Elise ceased going into the grand home high on the mountain. She also Johann insisted the wicked mom did not matter. Her displeasure had been an unlucky aspect, they informed themselves. They dismissed the harsh words along with the unpleasant thoughts. They pretended nothing might make in the way of the joyful and after. On festive days however, if there was a lot to observe, Elise frequently found herself lonely and waiting Johann paid his sanity and feted along with his loved ones. In these lonely minutes, Elise desired Johann to earn a decision but she did not dare ask, could not endure knowing he may not pick her.

There came a day after Elise discovered she had been taking Johann's kid. It had been an unanticipated but welcome boon. When she informed that the Johann, he explained that his heart was so complete that it ached.

He also offered his hand in marriage and also a spot in his realm, in his side. Elise told they would wait and watch. She wished to say. They started looking for a long run and if they found the physician and discovered the beating heart in the unborn child, they looked at one another and found they'd talk about one thing-- love. Johann and Elise were blinded by their own happiness, they shared with their great news using Johann's wicked mother that, on hearing the facts of a fresh air in the realm, a bastard heir, she stated, she kissed her eyes to challenging, black slits. She stated no child, a kid from two horribly distinct worlds, could be loved or recognized by anybody under her reign. Elise held her palms against her belly, tried to protect her precious furry child from these raw words. The wicked mother yells Elise from her house and Johann stood and said, torn between his mom and could be spouse. Elise expected to locate a way to forgive his excitement. She'd never forget.

It occurred on a Typical day filled with exceptional moments, daily when Johann painted the nursery a soft shade of pink to the kid who'd be a woman who'd be called Emma. He stood at the area admiring his job, imagining his girl holding his kid close to the massive window, possibly staring up in the skies. Elise stood at the kitchen preparing her guy a nice meal, humming for her infant, hoping in her pleasure. She had been overcome with a sudden, horrible pain at the chair of her uterus. It ended up being a pain so sharp and exact, she could not make one noise. The previous moment Elise recalled was falling into her knees and believing, "I can't bear to get rid of this." Johann discovered, on the ground, bleeding breathing shallow following their residence full of the odor of meat. They mourned the loss in their kid but rather than ripping them apart, their rue made them appreciate each other much better and more.

When she completed her research, Elise advised Johann she needed to leave the much Off location, away from anything. She was given a position where she had prepared her whole life. It was too difficult to reside among so many thoughts of exactly what should happen to be. She did not wish to raise kids in a location where its citizens could constantly look upon them more hers than his. Johann stated he knew. He explained they'd discover a way to enjoy each other over a hopeless space. She considered him. She trusted in her pleasure.

On the eve of her death, Johann sat alongside Elise onto a wooden dock. They Appeared outside on moonlit waters; their minds littered with wine. He explained the most gorgeous things she'd ever heard a guy say to a girl. He presented her with a ring, a gorgeous diamond in the form of a tear. He tried to slip the ring onto her hands but it didn't match. Elise laughed, nervously, stated it was a terrible omen. Johann stated they'd resolve the ring. He explained it was a detail, also details did not matter. He explained, please, take this ring, so please remain here, along with me, within my realm. Elise looked in the gorgeous ring and idea of the way she had never shared just how much she adored him. She wondered the way he left her forget all of the tragedies which had befallen her until he adored her.

Johann believed her tears supposed she was saying. Elise passed Johann his Ring, her hands shaking. She stated; I cannot remain; I can't believe you requested. She stated you don't understand me at all; these facts really do matter. She explained should Have asked if you can leave this place. Johann stated he'd never known any other sort of life. He said that these were his folks and that was his land. He said He'd spend his entire life leaving her love which property how he did,

His family would increase to take her. He grew mad, said she had been his, stated He'd never let her move. Elise held her belly, recalled the kid once Growing there and the way the reduction of her jump them together tightly. They sat Together in quiet, the nighttime air cooling between these. She Understood she'd been correct about fairy tales around along.

Chapter 13: From the Sleeping Apple

Once upon a time, there was a beautiful old apple tree in a beautiful garden. He was standing in a small village in Styria, whose name we do not reveal. As is customary, the apple tree was in full bloom every year and then produced many wonderfully fragrant apples of the variety "Crown Prince Rudolf."

Even our grandmothers knew this Styrian apple variety. They make many apple pies for their grandchildren out of it. Nothing is a proud ending to a ripe Styrian apple than to be processed by loving hands into baked apples, apple strudel, jams, or other goodies. It was also possible to make apple juice for the children and cider for the adults.

When the apples were ripe at the time of harvest, the first of them fell off the tree by themselves. Then people knew they had to get ladders and harvest apples. Meanwhile, the children played all sorts of games with the apples. They collected apples that had already fallen to the ground into large baskets. No one noticed that one of the most beautiful apples slept blissfully under the canopy and escaped all eyes. He dreamed of wonderful dreams that had nothing to do with apple compote or strudel dough. Some apples do not want to be enjoyed as cider, but watch the snowflakes dance or say good night to the night owl. You may want to travel once. But who asks an apple what he wants to do with his life?

Our red-cheeked apple refused to wake up from his blissful slumber. The tree that loves its fruits protected it with its foliage. It's just that an apple cannot stay on the tree forever. Gevatter Herbststurm will make sure of that someday. He zaust the apple tree many a day and plucking it from all leaves. Then it's over with the shelter for our apple dreamer. After all, Ms. Holle had a look in and one morning had the snowflake ballet dance. It was snowing and snowing. Our apple woke up from its slumber and was astonished. Since he was the only one left, our apple dreamer soon froze. So after a while, he fell into the soft snow bed. The blackbirds who were out of food thanked him for having been waiting for them.

Sleep-travel 16: Julia and the little dragon Ferdinand

Many children would like to have an animal, just like you. But many parents do not allow that. And most of the time they have good reasons. But when I was a little kid, I knew a girl named Julia. She was an only child and had no siblings. Little Julia wanted so much to have a dog as a playmate. But the strict father did not allow it.

Julia was so sad that she did not want to eat anything anymore. She often felt lonely. Dad and Mom worked all day. Julia often had to warm up the prepared lunch or go to grandma before she did her homework. Grandma Emmeli looked at her sad granddaughter and thought, "No, that will not work!". She took the girl by the hand and went with her into the forest. There she told the sad child of the little dragon Ferdinand. As a child, Granny was not allowed to have a cat or a guinea pig, although she longed for an animal. So, she had just invented a dwarf village and a little dragon named Ferdinand. Whenever she felt lonely, she imagined stories in her imagination playing in her dwarf village. The dragon Ferdinand was her best friend. Grandma had many adventures with him. Julia wanted to know from grandma where the little dragon had lived. "Well!"

Said Granny and laughed: "Under my blanket. The most secret of all places where my parents could not come. "Julia suddenly knew a solution to her problems.

A year later, Julia had a best friend named Anna-Lena. Grandma Emmeli wanted to know what they were playing. "That's secret!" Said Julia.

Sleep-travel 17: Paul and the dangerous weather witch

Paul is a little boy, just as old as you are. He can play for hours in the garden. Paul is happy about a rainbow as well as a curious mole. From computers and TVs, he holds nothing, because the garden is much more exciting. Paulchen can harvest late wild strawberries and discover hoarfrost on autumn leaves. Hedgehogs sometimes shuffle through the garden at dusk. They lick up the boiled potatoes with milk, which Paul has secretly put under a bush. Paul watches her from his skylight with the telescope.

But everything was bewitched this summer. It was raining when Paul wanted to go swimming. It was stormy-cold as soon as Paul put on his shorts. When he collected tadpoles from the stream to take them home in a jar, a thunderstorm suddenly came on.

"It's like bewitched this summer!" Scolded, Paul's father. So, Paul came to the conviction that a dangerous weather witch had to be involved. Of course, the adults had other explanations - but that does not matter. Parents cannot know everything. A weather witch can be very dangerous if left unattended. That's the same with young children. Both have only bad pranks in their heads. Small children, however, have no lightning, no steady rain, and no thunder at hand if they want to annoy others.

After Paul had identified the dangerous weather witch as the cause of his problems, he retired to his nursery. He was thinking about a spell to help. It would be great if the weather witch sends rain only at night and unlearns how to make a thunderstorm. Paul tried the spell "Peppery Rubbish Gigantic Rat Thundercrack Cockroach Lake," but nothing happened. He tried "Bumfiedel Drumbinatus Kakalimba Kink Break Frustoribum," but the new spell did not seem to work. The little boy fell asleep over it. But it was also tedious to keep a dangerous weather witch in check.

The next day was the beautiful autumn weather. Maybe one of the spells had worked. Paul moved to the pond with Brother Tobias and Neighbor's daughter Ella to catch tadpoles. Of course, he did not tell the two of the weather witch.

Sleep-travel 18: Princess Pinka and her castle

One day Princess Pinka went for a ride in her blue couch. From the carriage, Princess Pinka could see many beautiful things - a blue forest, for example, and many blue trees. Princess Pinka thought it was all very nice, but something was missing. Sometime later, the carriage stopped, and Princess Pinka paused. She stood on a blue hill and looked at the world.

But what was that? In the middle of the shimmering blue mountains, there was a small valley with a pretty castle. But this castle had an extraordinary color. There was a beautiful pink castle with a small, pink turrets and a large, pink meadow.

Princess Pinka wanted to have a close look at that. She went back to the carriage and continued on the drive. Princess Pinka was very excited. A pink princess lock she had always dreamed of.

She came closer to the castle - but wait, someone was sitting on a pink bench and looked very sad: a little pink princess. Princess Pinka stopped and got off the carriage. "Why are you looking so sad?" She asked the little pink princess. "Oh," said the little princess, "I cannot see all this anymore! Every night I dream of a blue castle, and whenever I wake it up, it's gone! "Princess Pinka's eyes widened. "Do you know what?" She said. "I'm exactly the other way around! I live in a blue castle. But every night I dream of a castle-like this one! "The little princess stood up and could hardly believe it. The two considered for a moment, then they exchanged their clothes and shoes and made their way to their new home. The little princess lived from now on content in the blue castle. Princess Pinka, however, was happy in her new, pink princess castle.

Chapter 14: Priorities

Jack was a 65-year-old man who was rather proud of the life that he had built for his family. Since his teenage years, he had worked hard and done everything he could over the past five decades to give his family the life he felt they deserved. He spent long hours working as a laborer, pulling in as many extra shifts as he could so that he could provide for his family. Thanks to his hard work, his wife was able to stay home and raise their three children in a beautiful home that he had purchased for them. He filled the home full of furniture, food, and various treasures based on whatever his family desired to have. When his family wanted to go on vacation, he would work overtime to afford the added expense and would always plan dreamy vacations that brought his family great joy. They would visit places like Disney Land, Martha's Vineyard, and even Arizona to see the desert. His family had traveled to many different places, enjoying all the different views and creating many different memories.

Although he seemed to be around fairly frequently, Jack never truly felt as though he was able to relax and enjoy his time with his family. He had grown so used to working hard that he always had to be doing something: fixing something, building something, cleaning something, or moving something around. No matter what day it was or how much work he had already done, Jack would always do more work than what was reasonable. He simply felt uncomfortable just sitting around and enjoying the presence of his family. To Jack, nothing felt more satisfying than retiring after a hard day of working and feeling the comfort of his pillow rising to meet him.

One day, when he turned 66, Jack found that he was not feeling as good as he used to. For a while, he chalked it up to being older and dealing with regular pains of old age. After a few months, however, Jack could no longer deny that he experienced some fairly serious symptoms. His symptoms had grown so strong that he could no longer do the labor that he once had, so he quit his job and retired to please his family. Jack would have found a way to keep working despite his setbacks with his health if it were up to him. Still, he listened and retired, as he knew he probably should.

Shortly into his retirement, even simple things became challenging for Jack. He could no longer work like he used to, and eventually, even smaller tasks like climbing the stairs or going for a walk to the mailbox became more of a challenge for him. Finally, with his family's insistence, Jack went to visit a doctor to see why he might be experiencing such hardship with his health. It was from that appointment that Jack went on to learn that he was terminally ill with cancer and that he had waited too long to be checked, so he was beyond the point of being able to be cured.

Jack and his family were shocked by this news as they realized that the once vital and virile man was quickly falling apart before their very eyes. Within weeks, Jack could no longer climb the stairs at all, and sometimes he even had trouble holding his coffee mug or pouring himself a glass of water. His wife, Susan, had to do everything for him. Being unable to do anything for himself made Jack angry and embarrassed, as he had always been a very proud and self-sufficient man. He spent the past five decades taking care of this woman; he did not feel as though he needed his wife to be taking care of him now.

As time went on, Jack's anger turned into sadness. His family would all visit him and bring their young children around, and everyone would play and get along like they always had. This time, though, Jack was forced to sit there and observe and partake in the conversation as he could no longer get up and find some work to do to keep himself busy. It was during these visits that Jack grew to understand just how much he had missed by being so deeply devoted to his work ethic and not spending enough time paying attention to his family. He realized he had missed countless birthdays, holidays, anniversaries, and even simple day-to-day memories because he was so absorbed in his need to work that he never truly sat down to enjoy his family until it was almost too late.

At first, Jack was angry with himself for not having spent more time with his family. He could not understand how foolish he had been by working so intensely and missing out on the majority of his children's and grandchildren's lives. Then, he became angry that he felt he had no choice but to work hard to give them the life he wanted them all to enjoy. Eventually, Jack found himself thanking his own life for giving him enough time to see what he had missed and for allowing him to make up for it now before it was too late.

One day, when he was talking to his son, Jack decided to offer him some advice about his work ethic. Jack said, "Son, when I was your age, my priorities were all wrong. I thought I had to work the hardest, be the best, and make the most money to make my family happy. Your mother told me she wanted me around more and wished I was there for the kids more, and I justified my actions by saying that I was there financially to support them. But that's not enough, son. In life, simply giving someone our money and hard work is not enough. If you truly want to be happy and live your best life, you take some time every day to sit with your kids and enjoy them. Never work so hard that you miss birthdays, anniversaries, or even just those special suppers each night. Be there for as many moments as you can, son, because believe me, one day, they will have all slipped by. I realize now my priorities were wrong, and I taught you wrong. The true priority you need to have in life is to provide for your family, not just finances. Prioritize the opportunity to provide them with your time, your attention, and your love. Believe me, son. It will make a world of difference."

Jack's son never forgot this story and went on to live by these words even long after Jack had passed. Jack's son went on to teach his children about the value of these priorities, and they went on to teach their children! Thanks to Jack and his hard work, his entire family was able to enjoy more quality time together for generations to come. He took the time to realize that prioritizing finances was not the only important thing in life. Time, attention, and love also mattered when it comes to providing for your family and truly taking care of them and yourself.

Chapter 15: Gigantic Balloon

You feel the excitement and nervousness in your restless body as you approach the gigantic balloon. Climbing into the wicker basket, you feel your heart flutter, and your stomach does a small flip.

You can smell the propane and hear the burning flame ready to power this balloon into the air. Holding onto the edge of the basket, you wait for your secure ascent into the air. Feeling the smooth wood beneath your hand, the drift of the slightest amount of heat from the balloon, the distant smell of a salty ocean. As the basket starts to rise, you feel how tense and achy your muscles are. You concentrate on grounding yourself as your body is being lifted to unknown heights.

Digging your toes down into the floor of the basket. Feeling your strong, sturdy ankles supporting you letting you know they won't waver; they will keep you steady.

Your legs feel alive as the muscles reflectively tense and relax as you ground yourself. As you rise even higher, you feel a shift in your body.

The fear of the flight is leaving you; instead, you feel an uplifting grace and peaceful presence.

Your body doesn't feel as heavy as it did moments ago.

The almost weightlessness you experience settles you. As you look around at the beautiful scenery, you continue to stabilize your body. You are relaxing your aching back, allowing the curves to blend into themselves.

Your stomach is settling down as you focus your thoughts on your breathing. Breathing in and expanding your lungs, delivering oxygen to your body, and breathing out, allowing your muscles to relax and await their next oxygen delivery.

As you breathe in and out slowly, you can relax your shoulders, neck, and finally, your mind.

As you continue relaxing and breathing, you can focus on the land growing smaller beneath you. Like the troubles, you leave behind when you sleep.

The balloon drifts peacefully, and you can see the ocean now. The water is deep blue, the beach overcrowded, and people are eager to find the blissful relaxation you're already experiencing.

The red and white umbrellas line the crowded beach, people lying on their towels on the warm sand. You're above the beach now, and people point, and you can hear them hoot and holler as you soar above.

Hearing the ocean lull beneath the sound of the crowd. You wave hello with a warm smile, thankful you can easily slip away from this crowded area and into your cocoon of happiness and warmth.

The balloon drifts further from the crowd and noises. The ocean is shrinking and becoming distant. You can no longer smell or hear the bustle that was on the ocean shore. Now, your mind is welcoming the quiet uninhabited lands you are approaching. Your nose is eager for the clean, crisp scents of the fields beneath you.

Seeing many colors of wildflowers blur together as you soar above. Like a bird in a lengthy flight for winter, you take in all your surroundings.

Relaxing, breathing, just being.

You are traveling away for your long, peaceful rest. Stepping away from the cold harshness that can sometimes be a reality, and traveling to the warm, sunny peace deep inside your mind. Below you see a laundry line and a small farmhouse; seeing the clothing dance on the line as you gently pass by as if now, they are waving to you as you waved to the beachgoers. The land turns from flat and uninhabited to small rolling hills with the occasional house.

You see, the town grows as you travel towards the center, roads, houses, and more businesses.

As the path of your life, you start fresh, not knowing many things, being able to see and know everything around you like the small farmhouse.

As you age, the roads you travel become familiar, but longer, more complicated, twists and turns, connecting to other roads. The houses keep popping up as you meet new people. The businesses are opportunities that you may latch onto or let them pass by, whichever is right for you at that time in your life. The connections throughout this town or city, working like your mind, often do. You are growing together, supporting a singular body.

You pass over neighborhoods, seeing the quiet towns below. Friendly neighbors have cookouts and children playing kickball together.

The towns pass by so quickly, and it reminds you of how quickly time can seem to pass. Your mind tries to distract you, remind you of the things you need to accomplish.

The things you need to worry about. It's time to quiet those thoughts.

You are creating your wind as you soar through the sky, whisper your concerns to the wind.

Let them travel through the air, fall to the ground. You can pick them up at another time. Whisper the thoughts of what you need to do tomorrow. Whisper the thoughts of what you should be worrying about.

Whisper anything that is on your mind. Watch the words leave your mouth, drift through your wind, fall to the ground. The words are jumbling together as they spiral to the ground. Falling and falling until you can no longer see them.

Those thoughts are gone now; you have freed your mind and have total control over your body.

Breathing in allowing your body to soak in the peace with a clear mind. Breathing out, feeling your body sigh with relief.

The hot air balloon is now traveling over the forest. The tops of the trees are green and lush. You feel like a cloud floating above the trees. The coverage dense in some areas, shielding you from the world below. While in other areas, it thins out, allowing you to peek at the wonderful mother nature has set before you.

A group of birds' flocks beside you can hear them calling out to each other at the curiosity you are presenting to them in this huge balloon.

How odd it must be for them. You look up and are again amazed at how a little bit of heat and this huge material are allowing you to soar with birds. The rainbow color panels seem to glow as the sun shines down through them.

The red panel was making you think of love and warmth. The orange panel was reminding you of tropical colors on an island, the flowers, the clothes, the fruits, and the peaceful setting sun.

The yellow panel reminds you of pure happiness and joy, like a full warm sun, or the tart bite of a lemon.

The green panel is showing the reflection of life; of mother nature as it surrounds you...the green of the trees, the grass, the fields below.

The blue panel, reflecting on the open, clear skies.

Open like your mind, absorbing the welcoming warmth of the other colors.

The purple panel reflects its vibrant color that can be rarer than the others and is often a sign of nobility—reflecting the rare peace and calm of complete bliss, reflecting this journey in this hot air balloon.

The forest is thinning out, and you can see a beach in the distance. As you approach it, you find yourself approaching a barely sandy and more rocky shore, the water angrily lapping at the shoreline.

While not friendly for a relaxing day at the beach, the sounds of the crashing waves reflect that of your beating heart. It's as if you can feel those waves beating against the rocks from deep within your soul.

You feel the blood pumping through your body, then beating through your heart. The waves are rolling in and out like your breath and working together to create a beautiful rhythm that is essential for your life.

The ocean's sounds start to drift off until you only feel your heart, mirroring what you know the ocean is doing even in your absence.

You approach an open field; you know your journey must be near its end. As the balloon starts to descend, you feel yourself falling slightly more horizontal.

I was peacefully drifting into the proper place of relaxation.

Your body shifts, finding the most comforting position as you feel the weight returning to your body.

The heaviness is weighing your body down until it feels impossible to do nothing but let it pull you down. Relax into the weight.

Feel your body sinking into the warmth of the descent. Allow your tired legs to rest, pulling the rest of your body down with them. Breath in and out slowly as you drift down into peace, lying your head back and feeling gravity welcome you home.

The warmth of the balloon envelopes you as you caress the ground. The balloon is at rest. Lie here as long as you like. Rest, breathe in the field around you.

What does this field look like up closely?

Are its fragrant flowers?

Warm and mellow wheat?

Close your eyes and rest for a moment.

Allow your body to sink in and enjoy this complete relaxation this trip has brought you. Reflect on the sights that you have seen, and only one thing stirs you from your revelry... The pilot asks you, "Do you want to go up again?"

Chapter 16: Alone on the Moon

Before we begin this journey downwards into the deepest realms of our sub-conscious, let us take a minute to physically and mentally and spiritually acclimate ourselves into being with an awareness of our inner sanctum, our internal workings. We will begin by going to a place of comfort, ideally a bed, or a very comfortable reclining chair, and we will relax our bodies to the furthest extent possible. Now, close your eyes, staying firmly on your back, with your arms relaxed at your sides and your legs rested downwards. Take one deep breath in your nostrils, counting slowly to four, and one deep breath out, through your nostrils again, counting slowly to four. Breathe in the breath of the spirit and breathe out the stress of the day. Now is the time to rest. Become aware of nothing but the air flowing through your nostrils, envision a steady flowing stream, smooth inhalations, and exhalations; your body becomes weightier and more relaxed with each passing cycle of breath. Allow your thoughts to become completely still. You focus on your core, your solar plexus, allowing your thoughts to flow outwards past your vision until they escape your being while only holding and retaining the pure awareness of spirit holy serenity of the mind and body. Breathe in, one, two, three, four, then breathe out, one, two, three, four, each breath becoming slower. One... two... three... four... One... two... three... four... One... two... three... four... One... two... three... four... One... two... three... four... One... two... three... four... Continue this pattern of breath, expanding, and sink deeper into yourself, becoming a voyeur of your own still, relaxed body, lost in time. Become lost in this experience as you journey further into the trance, and prepare for the road we are about to embark upon. Draw further and further away from your still, lying body, and into the realm of imagination, where images grow, the land of dreams that you are about to become one with. Erase your mind of all that is within it currently, and prepare the landscape for a new and fresh experience, in the farther reaches of reality. One... two... three... four... inhale... One... two... three... four... exhale... One... two... three... four... inhale... One... two... three... four... exhale... Now, with your mind, body, and spirit rested, entranced, and fertile, let us begin.

You find yourself on the surface of the moon. You are alone. You move your body. Everything feels ethereally heavy as if you are as big as the universe, yet light, as if there is barely any pull towards the ground. You jump up and stay up, and fall slowly to the ground. You scream. No sound is heard. You scream again, as loud as you can. All the rage you have ever felt, any fear or any negative feeling that has ever crossed your path in this eternal life comes pouring out of you in one giant scream. Yet there is nothing. There is no mark made on this atmosphere by your pain, for there is no atmosphere, for you are alone, on the moon. With the silent scream, go your memories. Just as your scream went silent on this surface, meaningless and less than it ever did in your known reality back on planet earth, too does any negative feeling that came with it. Everything begins to evaporate here, as now there is only you, alone, weightless and free. You jump up and down and up and down, making incredible bounds with each leap. You are floating, flying, across a surface hitherto unimaginable by the average human. Very few people have ever been here, and you are now one of them. Whereas they had to wear very large and heavy and intricate suits, guard against the elements, and breathe, you are naked. You can breathe effortlessly as if the deprivation of oxygen has been replaced with a breath of spirit that charges your entire body in an even greater sense than the oxygen of the earth. Every breath you take is like ten breaths that activate parts of your body that you have never felt before. You are leaping, incredibly, up and up into the air, then, leisurely, falling ever so slowly down. You kick, and wave, and flip around. It is like being in the middle of the ocean, yet vacant, and clear, and black. Grey rock spreads before you as far as you can see, in every direction. Gigantic mountains give way into even larger craters as if the pores and hairs on the skin of some great stone deity. You feel the vibration from this deity course through you, silent, with no sound. Yet there is a feeling, and this feeling, in its own right, is louder than any sound you have ever heard, or could ever hope to make. It is pure spirit, charging through you. All around you is black, and stars, closer than they have ever been in your memory. The stars are larger, like fireflies, floating in the pure black sky. And there is the earth, your memories, now so very far away, as to be almost meaningless. But it is beautiful. You feel so removed from it now, yet you can bask in its beauty in a way you never thought possible. The great blue planet, a blue orb unto itself, alone in the cosmos, so far away from any neighbor; so far away from you. You think about your life there. Like picking up a handful of sand, the grains slowly pass through your fingers. There is much subjectivity in life and such a changing of being. Your environment so defines your environment, yet your environment is so temporary and so prone to change. What you know as life on earth couldn't exist here naturally. That being the biology, the skin, the flesh, the blood, the organs, everything that comprises what you have hitherto known to be life. Yet, here you are, beyond all this physiological being, a being of pure spirit, boundless, defying all laws of physics, transcending the existence that you had previously been indebted to, becoming something new, unknown, yet knowing itself, through the experience, feeling mysterious yet familiar. With infinite of leaps behind you, the earth has come and gone a million times, and you come upon the base of one of those great, gray mountains that had been in the distance. Time has passed into oblivion, yet you are still here. No hunger, no pain, no fear. You are to traverse up this mountain; you know it in your heart. You take the first leap, then the second, and you're climbing, climbing at the speed of light. Dust and rocks fly behind you, with every landing, with every spring of the foot. You feel as if the whole mountain could crumble beneath you, so you become gentle more and more, careful, as it is your responsibility, if you so choose, to keep this mountain as it exists, tall, reaching up from the surface into the heavens it came from. Softly, you continue up the mountain, making large strides, until, there you are, at the top. You feel as if you might just float off into space, but some small force is keeping your feet tethered to the ground if they want to be. You twirl around, your arms out in front of you, and you can see what seems to be the moon's entire surface, even though that would be impossible. You see the edges rounding down into the globe, each crater, every lump of rock, every other mountain, yet this is the largest, and you are the master of it. You jump up as high as you can, and it seems as if you are a mile above the peak. You twirl, and twirl, as slow as you can, spinning in slow motion as you float like a feather, slowly, slowly, back down to the peak. The tip of your foot touches the highest point, and you balance there, forever, the earth coming and going and coming and going as you stand in this balance, effortlessly, free, nothing pushing or pulling on your being, just you, still, there. After several lifetimes, you feel the urge to go back down the mountainside, so you roll forward, and begin to tumble, like a tumbling weed in the wind, all the way down. With every bounce, you are ten feet in the air, and, before you know it, you have reached the familiar plateau of the surface, and there you are, with one final bounce, rested on the flat of the moon. You lay there for as long as you were at the top, several more lifetimes, still, in the lone, empty, black, and white void. There is nothing. And then you fall asleep.

Chapter 17: The Private Isle

Take a deep breath and close your eyes. Imagine now that you are walking on a sandy beach. The beach has beautiful, white sand, and you can feel it between your bare toes. Every step that you take is like a soft pillow; the sand gently conforms to the shapes of your feet, perfectly balancing your feet and supporting your steps. The sand is incredibly fine and silky as it moves around, and it is warmed by the sun's gentle rays that beam down from the sky. Some of the steps that you take are onto the sand that has been gently caressed by the ocean's water lapping up on shore, and the texture is a little bit different. The sand feels firmer where it is wet, holding its shape more with the water that soaks through it.

A gentle breeze goes by, warm and wet, and tasting faintly of the ocean. It glides through your hair, and you notice that your shirt gently ripples around you, softly rubbing against your skin. It is a simple, but soft cotton, lightweight and breezy as it tugs around you, and looking down, you realize that it is your favorite color. You have soft shorts on as well, and you are walking barefoot along the beach. There is no one there with you; for miles and miles around, all you can see is the sand, the water, the sky, and the greenery.

The sun warms your body, first heating up your hair, and then your skin. It is not too hot on this day as you walk along the beach, you notice; in fact, it is the perfect temperature for a relaxing stroll to the cadence of the gentle waves of the water lapping up at the shore. You see the cleanest, bluest sky you have ever seen—it is a vibrant, warm, inviting shade of blue, and there are little wisps of white clouds, barely there, floating above the gentle wind. They are high up in the sky, just barely breaking up the otherwise even shade of blue everywhere that you can see.

You look to your left, and you can see a dense tropical jungle just beyond the sand. Palm fronds shoot up toward the sky from long, spindly tree trunks like a tuft of a lion's tail, leaning over the sand and spreading themselves out as much as they can to soak up the life-giving rays from the sun above. They are the most verdant green that you have ever seen, and each frond is covered in wide blades that seem to curl upwards, ever-reaching out for the sun. Amidst the base, where all of the fronds come together atop the trunk, you see several rounds, oblong fruits, nearly the color of a lime. They are coconuts growing above you, and each tree seems to house several of them bunched together. Along with the bases of the trees, you can see dense growth of bushes stretching out, flourishing underneath the sun. They are wide, leafy, and bushy, and you cannot quite tell what they are, but they are even greener, somehow than the coconut leaves that were dotting the sky above you.

You continue to walk along the quiet beach, step by step. Although you are alone, you do not feel bad at all. You love the quiet solitude as you walk along, and the solitude is there to help you as you go along the way. It is quiet but not too quiet, and you feel at ease, comforted by the waves that you pass by. Soon, you decide to move out from the beach. You move toward the greenery that fills the center of the island. As you go along your way, you see that the bright wall of dense green is just a wall of bushes that have thrived underneath the sun. Beyond the bushes, you can see that the ground is quite walkable, so you continue along.

As you step past the bushes, the air immediately changes. What was once warm and smelling of the sea was suddenly much cooler. The shift from the sun to shade was immediately noticeable, but it is still pleasantly comfortable, you are pleased to notice. It is like a whole new world on the other side of the greenery, and as you look around, you realize that you are surrounded by all sorts of wildlife up in the trees. Though they are all carefully out of sight, you can hear that they are all around you. You hear the hundreds of birds singing their songs all around you. You can see the shadow of a bird on the ground beneath you, but every time you look up, they are gone.

Inside the forest, you notice that some many fronts and ferns grow closer to the ground. They are a darker green than the green of the plants that are out in the constant sunlight, but they are beautiful in their ways. You see how some of the fronds, heavy with the leaves' blades, hang down toward the ground.

The ground underfoot has changed, too. It is soft beneath your feet, but in an earthy, loamy way instead. It no longer sinks underneath your weight, though you can feel that it still has some give. The ground is cool and slightly damp underneath your toes, a sharp contrast from the sand that you had been on just moments prior.

You continue to wander aimlessly throughout the jungle forest. Everywhere that you look, it is more of the same, but constantly changing. There are endless plants and branches, but they are endlessly arranged in different manners. Soon, you see a rock. The rock is the perfect size to sit on and even is shaped vaguely like a natural seat. You take it, marveling at the smoothness of the stone underneath your hands, and let your hand run over its flawless surface. For rock, it is surprisingly comfortable, and you allow yourself to sit on it and close your eyes, listening to the jungle's song.

You hear the sounds around you, first as just one endless cacophony around you. It is almost too busy to comprehend, and it all gets bunched up into one sound: Jungle. But you can break it up into other sounds, too, if you stop to listen closer. You hear the gentle buzzing of insects all around you, creating the undertone to the entire symphony of sounds that you hear. The gentle undertone of the buzz from the cicadas is punctuated by the occasional chirp of a bird that is nearby. It is high-pitched, but not harsh on the ears; it is a loud chirping that comes in three each and every time that you hear it pass by. The wind blows through the leaves above you gently, creating a ripple of leaves rubbing against each other. Occasionally, you hear what sounds like a monkey's cry, somewhere in the distance, and some chattering of another animal nearby.

Soon, you can hear different birds, too, all singing together. You can hear the soft, trilling song of a bird on the right, high, lilting, and soothing. You can hear a slightly harsher sound to your left, but it is not unpleasant as it sings to you. The songs of the birds all complement each other perfectly. The more you listen, the more layers you seem to uncover in the ever-changing song around you. You can hear the sound of a frog croaking now and then, punctuating the birds' melodies.

Underneath all of it, however, you hear something else: the unmistakable sound of water babbling over rocks. There must be some sort of stream or river nearby. You feel compelled to go toward the sounds, and you are on your feet before you think about it. You open your eyes, which have been closed all along, and then you realize that you can see the wildlife that you had been blinded to when you had first entered the great jungle. You have grown accustomed to the sights around you, and you find that it is much easier to spot everything around you, and suddenly, you can see all of the beautiful, colorful birds that surround you. You can see them all, hiding in the trees.

Listening closely, you think that you can follow the sound of the river as it flows past the rock. You follow it, feeling compelled to discover where it is and then head off to locate it. You are looking everywhere that you can for the source of the sounds, and you think that you have found it. Each step moves with more purpose as you go toward the sound, and soon, you see it.

There is a small stream of water, bubbling over smooth stones in every shade of grey that you can imagine. There is not much water there; only a few inches, and it would be easy to walk through it simply. On the other side of the stream, you can see that there is a pathway that seems to follow it, and you decide to cross. As you step into the water, you can feel it flow over your feet, cool and refreshing as it does. It laps around your toes as you walk carefully and with purpose across the stream. The rocks within it are smooth but noticeably bumpy as you go over them, and soon, you are over the stream altogether.

The trail takes you on a winding path that follows the stream's course, and the further you follow it, the more the stream seems to flow. As you walk, you can see it slowly swell up in power, and you realize that you must be getting closer to the water source. As you continue, you hear the sound of water becoming louder and louder, and soon, you are walking alongside what appears to be a cliff, with the ground on one side of you and the water on the other. You follow it around a bend, and you see it: A waterfall.

It is at least ten feet tall, and the water cascaded over the ledge, creating a current bubbling right underneath it. The water appears white at the base, very quickly fading into the deep blue of the river that the stream had eventually become. You are not sure how far you have walked, but it was a long way, and looking up at the sky, you realize that the sun is beginning to go down. It is time to make the long journey home.

Chapter 18: The Moonlit Garden

Imagine that you have just woken up. The sky is still dark, and upon glancing at your clock, you see that it is very late at night. Your entire home is sleeping, and you cannot hear a single thing. The silence is almost deafening over you, and you slowly swing your legs over the side of the bed, pushing yourself up to standing. You decide that what you need is a quick walk so you can fall back asleep without any problems.

Your bedroom carpet is plush underneath your feet—it is squishy and soft, giving each step and dampening the sounds under each step. Slowly and quietly, so as to not wake anyone else in your home, you make your way to the door to your home, compelled to keep walking by some unknown force or desire. You feel like you need to keep walking, so you do, quietly noticing the way that your body moves when you let it. It is loose, unencumbered by the stress or tension of the day. You feel perfectly relaxed as you move, and you know that you are going to exactly where you need to be.

You leave your home and quietly shut the door behind you. The nighttime is alive and abuzz with the sounds of everything else that, like you, are awake amidst the darkness. But, on that night, it is not particularly dark; the sky, and the world beneath it, is brightly illuminated by the biggest full moon that you have ever seen, made brighter by the faint haze of a wispy cloud that hangs over it at that moment in time. However, that cloud would not remain in place for very long, for the wind is gently blowing around you, and you can see that, just beyond the cloud is nothing but the clear night sky.

In the distance, you can hear the buzzing sounds of crickets chirping around you. They sing their songs loudly and boldly, and you decide that, since you have nothing better to do on that late night, you will walk toward it. You follow the chirping of crickets, punctuated only by the occasional soft hoot of a bat, or the billowing of wind through the leaves. You walk through grass, which is cool and soft beneath your feet, and tickles between your toes a bit as you go. You pass through the yard to an area lined with trees, and you keep going past them. You keep on moving, and soon, you approach what appears to be a garden. The garden is in a vast clearing that is lined by a wave of trees that appeared to have been grown there intentionally. The trees are lined up, creating a wall against the nighttime sky, but above you, you can still see the moon hanging in the air. The moon is no longer obscured, you quietly note to yourself, and the cloud seems to have disappeared completely. Instead, you see what looks like thousands of stars all overhead. You can see what appears to be a purplish streak, almost cloudy in appearance, throughout the sky, and you know that it is the Milky Way galaxy.

You stop and marvel at the sky for a moment. You rarely get a moment to disconnect, stop, and look at the sky truly, but at that moment, you have that. You have nothing pressing to be dealing with, and you have no reason not to try to enjoy the stillness of the night around you, reveling in its quiet calmness in a way that you cannot do amidst the hustle and bustle of daily life.

Before long, you hear a sound behind you, a quiet rustling in the flowers that grow across the ground, and you turn to look at them. There is nothing there but the wind, but with it came the soft, sweet scent of roses and the other flowers perfuming the air around you.

You walk toward the flowers, kneeling when you get to them.

The first plant that you see is a beautiful rosebush. You can see that the buds are beginning to open up, and a few flowers appear to have already opened up entirely. The soft, silky petals are the color of the sunset. They are orange-ish in the center, and they fade into a soft, satiny pink color at the tips, beautifully and warmly. Just like the sunset, they bring to you feelings of comfort and peace, as well as a feeling of finality. They are soothing and welcoming, and you begin to feel a bit sleepy as you run your fingers across the delicate petals of the rose.

You look over, and you can see that the garden is filled with endless different flowers, ranging greatly from type to type. Some flowers are light pink and growing in bunches, straight up from the stems. Some are purple and delicate, swinging in the breeze. Others are red, and others still are yellow. You look around the garden, and you can see that each and every flower is a different color. You can see that they all come together, carefully planted at just the right distance apart, so they can all grow, and there is not a weed in sight. The entire garden must be well maintained, and you tell yourself as you look around.

You settle down to look at the flowers around you, enjoying the gentle garden that you are surrounded by, and then you see something. As another warm, gentle breeze blows past you, you see something light up, and then another something and another something after that. There are fireflies gently rising up and out of the garden into the sky above it. They flash their beautiful colors, each of them existing in a different color altogether. Some are brighter, and others are dulled considerably. Some yellows flicker and shine like incandescent streetlights that move about, up and down, and side to side. Some greens appear to be bright green, the color of neon lights. Others still look red and pink. They are all vastly different colors, and they all dance in the air the flowers.

You sit and watch their intricate dances as they buzz about each other, the lights seeming almost to pulse as they float on the gentle breeze. The sounds of their buzzing are gentle in the air, and it harmonizes with the chirps of the crickets and the drone of the katydids in the distance. You enjoy their private show, reveling in the secrecy of it all and enjoying the gentle swaying of the insects as they go.

Occasionally, you see a moth drift through the fireflies, and the fireflies all clear the way, creating a wave of darkness as the moth drifts past. Still, beyond that, not a single animal comes to visit as you watch the show until you notice something else: You hear the sound of a gentle hoot behind you.

Turning around, you see an owl staring at you. It is perched atop a low-hanging branch near you. The owl has a warm, brownish plumage, mottled in colors of yellowish, cream, and darker brown. Its head is smooth and has a white, heart-shaped face with two big, brown eyes that stare closely at you. The owl's beak appears small, almost tucked away, and all you can see, shining in the moonlight, is its face. It tilts its head as you meet its gentle gaze, and you can see that it seems to be considering what you want. It is curious about you, almost lazily, so as it watches you as if silently telling you to get a move on with it already.

However, before you can do something, the owl suddenly spreads its wings to reveal the massive wingspan that it has, and it crouches down. You can see the power in its body as it pushes off from the branch, hard enough to make it dip down and wave helplessly in the air as an impressive stroke of wings lifts the owl into the air. It flaps its wings harder and harder, and yet, you do not hear a single sound—the flapping sound that you are accustomed to hearing in the daytime when a bird passes by is entirely silent as the owl goes overhead, treating you to the sight of its white body, speckled lightly with greys and creams on the chest as it flies away.

You are left, in awe, of the sight that you have seen, but you are also beginning to feel incredibly sleepy. All of that energy that you had from when you had woken up seems to have left you, and suddenly, you feel that intense urge to sleep fall over you. You are ready to sink back into your bed, so off you go after one last glance at the fireflies in their dance. You allow the memory of the fireflies to seal in your memory and off you go, retracing the steps you took. Occasionally, you notice the owl flying overhead as if it is guarding over you as you return home. It goes from tree to tree, flying out of sight, but always returning to you.

When you arrive back at your door, you look over your shoulder one last time. Perched on the railing to your porch, you see the owl. It is looking at you, black eyes gleaming in the light from your porch, and it tilts its head. You get the feeling that it is laughing at you, or at least, it would be if owls could laugh, and you feel yourself smile as you turn the cool doorknob in your hand. You debate saying something, but you are not sure that you knew what you were looking at, and you were even less sure that you knew that the owl was even able to understand you. Instead, you settle for a slight dip of your head in acknowledgment to the owl, and you find yourself pleasantly surprised when it nods its head right back to you in return. Was its coincidence or intentional? You may never know, but that's okay.

You make your way upstairs and into your bed, pleased to notice that no one else had woken up during your midnight romp through the garden, and you slip into bed. The mattress feels more inviting than it ever was before as you find just the right spot for you. You feel your body melting into the bed, releasing all of the tensions that you did not realize that you had, and you relax. With a deep breath in and out, you feel yourself calming down. You feel warm and comforted, more than ever before. You feel the waves of tiredness coming over you, little by little, and quietly, in the comfort of your bed, you drift right back to sleep.

Conclusion

In this life, there is nothing more important than a good night's rest. It is was decides whether or not tomorrow will be good or great. Everyone deserves sweet dreams, sound sleep, and a refreshed mind when they wake. I have written these stories with the design that each one will intrigue you, inspire you, and entertain you. My hope is that while reading this book, you will not just find the chance for a great night's sleep. I hope that you also find the chance for a new perspective. Dreams are what dictate how we respond and react in the days that follow. Positive dreams lead us to respond positively. Negative dreams leave us wonting the time comes. If you're struggling to sleep and desire to find peace, there is no better way to dictate your night than through a bedtime story. Through these stories, you can not only send yourself drifting off to sleep swiftly. By choosing the story that fits your mood best, only you will know, you can lull yourself into the slumber that will match your next day. Big day at the office tomorrow? Want a go-getter attitude? Pick a story that's inspiring! Having a soothing day at the park or a hike through the forest? Pick one of the more zen pieces in this collection. There is no limit to the power you can hold over your dreams and your life. But the best way to take control of your life is to take control of your sleep. And the best way to take control of your sleep is to start with a tranquil and enchanting bedtime tale that will carry you to another land.

The next step is to tuck yourself in and focus on your dreams. Your mind is your temple. Treat it properly. Fill it with hope, inspiration, and wonder. Magic is not gone from your world or life. You're full of it and life is of it. It's all there for the taking. And so is a peaceful night's rest and a sound mind.

There are many things on the mind and we just want to settle down into some warm blankets and wrap ourselves in cozy dreams. It's a respectable desire that we all share. Unfortunately, sometimes our minds and our desires are not always on the same platform. They can travel along the same route but can be arriving at the destination at different times and on different schedules. Simply put, we don't always have the control we deserve. But this book is written for folks like you in mind. Someone who wants to send themselves off to sleep with fantasy and wonder as their guides. Or maybe you are someone who has trouble falling asleep? If you are looking for a comforting and peaceful collection of tales to guide you to your realm of dreams, this is the book for you. There is intrigue in these stories, yes. There is excitement and growth, as well. And there are also the key elements needed to soothe the mind and soul into a sound night of slumber. You don't have to wait all night for your body to catch up with your desires. If you want to drift off at will, simply choose your favorite tale and read away.

CPSIA information can be obtained
at www.ICGtesting.com
Printed in the USA
LVHW021709151120
671608LV00011B/658

9 781801 184991